PERSONAL PERSPECTIVES

by the same author

MANCHESTER:
A CELEBRATION

Brian Redhead

PERSONAL PERSPECTIVES

ANDRE DEUTSCH

All the following articles first appeared in *Saga Magazine*
between 1984 and 1994

First published in Great Britain in 1994 by
André Deutsch Limited
106 Great Russell Street
London WC1B 3LJ

Second impression October 1994

CIP data for this title is available from the British Library

ISBN 0 233 98906 4

Printed and bound in Great Britain by
WBC, Bridgend, Mid Glam.

FOREWORD

We had already begun planning *Personal Perspectives* before Brian fell ill and, as always, he was tremendously enthusiastic about the project. Reading through his articles he remarked upon the development of his own particular style of writing over the preceding decade; indeed, fuelled with ambition he had decided to embark upon his memoirs during the forthcoming summer months.

We believe Brian was unique and his style so individual and distinctive that only his personal recollections and embellishments written in his inimitable persona would do him justice. That is why there will be no official biography, but we are fortunate to have this collection of articles as a reminder of the man himself.

Some of the proceeds of the book will go to Brian's favourite charities.

Abby Redhead

CONTENTS

A New Look at Old Age

When I was forty-five I was forever talking about retirement. 'Only another fifteen years,' I would say. But I never continued . . . 'and then I shall . . .'

I wasn't thinking that far ahead. I was simply looking for an escape without having the courage to do anything about it.

And then fate took a hand. I was fired. And far from being affronted, I was overjoyed. It was not just a relief, it was a release, a new release of life. I was free to make my living in the way I had always wanted but had never dared. Today, ten years later, I never mention retirement. I am no longer postponing the change.

Of course I am lucky to be able to live what is called the freelance life, doing this and that, rather than one salaried job. But the real point of the freedom is not that you cease to be a wage slave but that you cease to be the slave of the timetable.

Let me explain.

There is only now. The past is what we can remember now of what went before. The future is what we can speculate now about what may happen next. But the only reality is the present. And happiness is the pursuit not of future rewards but of the perfection of the moment.

The most moving letter I have ever read in a newspaper was from a man who wrote to the *Daily Mail* to say that he had denied his wife countless pleasures during his working life that they might enjoy them together in retirement. 'I retired last week,' he wrote. 'She died yesterday.' He was desolated. He knew he had been mean. Now there was no way in which he could make amends.

I am not suggesting that we should live a life of wanton and

1

immediate pleasure with no thought for the future. Prudent provision for old age to provide not only for necessities but the necessary comforts is essential. But no less important is the prudent appreciation of the present, of living each day to the full. If you postpone that, it might never happen. And retirement will be a let-down.

You are what you are not what you do. When you leave an occupation, reach a certain birthday, pass an anniversary which the state has decreed marks you down as a pensioner, you should not be diminished. Now is the time to be yourself.

Of course it helps if there has been prudent provision. It is disturbing to find the Secretary of State for Social Services whimpering about the cost of pensions. Retirement for men at sixty is too expensive, he says. And in forty years' time the number of people with state pensions will rise by a third while the number at work and paying national insurance will hardly change, he says. In which case they will have to pay more, won't they?

The old are not another species. They are us, now or later.

An inadequate pension is not good enough. It should rise in relation to earnings and not to inflation. Indeed, I was glad to see that it was a Conservative MP, Andrew Bowden, who questioned the relevance of the retail price index to the pensioner's spending. Mr Bowden, who is chairman of the all-party group for pensioners, pointed out that pensioners spend proportionately more on housing, food, and heating than other people. 'I suspect,' he said, 'that the way the RPI is calculated in no way reflects the costs of pensioners.'

I sometimes think the Government should take the number they first thought of and then add ten per cent in calculating pension increases. It all goes back into the economy and it would not cripple the nation.

But perhaps governments, like proud old ladies who fail to take up their benefits, still think of social security as charity. Yet it is no more charity than the donation from the Civil List to the Royal Household.

It is the way in which we have chosen to conduct the nation's finances. And it is as wrong for old people to fail to receive that to which they are entitled as it is for public money to be misappropriated. Age Concern, among others, is doing its best to see that nobody goes wrongly short.

It is sensible too that the Government has finally decided to do something about portable pensions. I have long thought that everyone should have a private pension fund, lodged perhaps with a building society. Three people should contribute to it – the employer, the employee, and the state.

If you change your job, you go on contributing, so does the state, and the new employer chips in. In lean times you pay what you can. In good times as much as you can. And when you come to draw the pension, the state tops it up, if it is inadequate, and if it is more than sufficient, you pay tax as you do on any other income.

But, as I say, there is more to life than money. Proper pension arrangements to provide food and housing and heating should be the accepted norm. Anything less is failure. Old age should command richer rewards.

It is precisely at the time when your days are numbered that you should not count the days. The timetable is irrelevant. What matters is to take each day as it comes. That of course is true at any age, but it may take a long time to learn that lesson. And old age, above all, is the time to put it into practice.

They used to call it wisdom. And they looked to the old to provide it.

Autumn 1984

Public Convenience

I went to the local post office the other day only to find that they had run out of stamps. When I reported this unprecedented event to my wife, she said: 'You are lucky they hadn't run out of post offices.' The plan to close several hundred sub-post offices up and down the country has provoked discontent nationwide. As one old gentleman in my village put it: 'If we don't agitate now, we shall be very agitated later.'

And he is right. Perhaps rather more right than he realises. The local post office is the pensioner's lifeline. It will be a matter of considerable inconvenience and hardship if it is closed. In the country it will necessitate travelling to another village and in the town journeying to another suburb. And it is good to see that pensioners both in towns and villages are organising their protestations, signing petitions, writing to their MPs.

But the threatened closure of local post offices is more than a matter of public inconvenience. It is a serious affront to civilised living. The local post office is not simply an office where pensioners collect their entitlements, it is the place where they report their continued presence in this world.

Going to the post office is a public act, and every human being to fulfill his or her humanity needs a public life as well as a private life.

The local post office is an arena where the community meets. It is a corner shop with royal assent, an important institution in our unwritten constitution. When a pensioner appears there to collect his or her benefit, he or she is saying: 'This is me, and I matter.'

The number of local post offices in the land cannot be determined to suit the convenience of the Post Office's accounting system. They can be determined only by the genuine demand of the community. To close a post office, without the consent of the community, is not only to diminish that community but to diminish the lives of those who adorn that community.

It is very important that the old should not be hidden away. Retirement should not mean withdrawal. A vigorous community requires the public presence of all its citizens, old as well as young. That is why those about to retire have to think very carefully about where to live. It is too easy to make for the little bungalow beside the seaside and then find yourself, as it were, living in an annexe to the real world, comfortable but unengaged.

If you are going to live elsewhere when you retire it is often better to make the move early, in advance of the date of your retirement, both to get to know where you are going to live and to get known. But it is often better still to stay put among relatives and friends and acquaintances. A friend of mine who lives and works abroad came home last winter to see his parents-in-law. He found the old couple huddled in a chilly house, unhappy and unwell. They could afford neither adequate heating nor many of the other legitimate comforts of old age. But they did own the house they lived in which they planned to leave to their three daughters.

My friend tried to devise a scheme whereby instead of waiting till they died and bequeathing their house to the children, they gave it to them now but continued to live in it rent free. Meanwhile the children borrowed money against the value of the house which they gave in regular instalments to the old couple to provide them with additional comforts.

You can guess what happened. The scheme foundered on family bickering and the old couple will shiver again this winter.

But the idea was right. And I am delighted to see that more and more finance houses are devising means by which old people can enjoy in their lifetimes the wealth accumulated in the ownership of their own homes. They reckon that at least a million old people could benefit from the release of capital from their homes. The schemes so far on offer fall far short of ideal – it is always prudent to be wary in dealing with money lenders – but I think the building societies who are anxious to expand their activities will soon come up with better schemes. The Government could usefully give them a prod. It is generous of the old to want to leave something to their descendents, but it is more important that they should live their last years in reasonable comfort.

Nor would I deny retired people perks. If for no better reason than to cock a snook at the Government, several local authorities are introducing extensions of schemes to provide cheaper travel or even free travel for pensioners. And British Rail is extending the benefit of the senior citizen rail card to men from the age of sixty.

There are those who tut-tut at such social generosity. It is, they say, another example of shameful hand-outs. Better a better pension. But that I think is too lofty a view. It would indeed be a far better world if every old person was guaranteed a pension large enough not only to provide the essentials of food and shelter but also some of the expected luxuries too. Perhaps that day will come. But in the meantime let the pensioners have a perk or two as well to facilitate their public life.

It is not enough to sit at home, albeit warm and well-fed, in front of the television. There is a further dimension in life, and I don't mean *even* for the old, I mean *especially* for the old – the public dimension, the emblem of your presence. If a free bus pass makes all the difference between getting out and about and staying in and keeping yourself to yourself, then I am all for it.

The editor of this magazine, I know, was much taken by a paragraph in a recent article in the Sunday Times about bull-fighting. 'What you can never explain to Spaniards,' said the author, 'is that while death is inevitable, you don't have to die straight away. You can always hang around, take the pension, and become the life and soul of Saga Holidays.'

There is a lot to be said too, for being the life and soul of the local post office.

Winter 1984

6

Accumulated Wisdom

At a Christmas Carol Concert in the church where the Brownings were married and Byron baptised, I found myself in procession alongside my friend and colleague on 'Today', John Timpson. 'I never thought I would walk down the aisle with you,' he whispered.

The two Davids, Owen and Steel, must often think the same, especially as each seems to be the bridesmaid and never the bride, for the electorate keeps putting them in second place and seldom first. Perhaps they should change the name of their Alliance to the Auld Alliance, not because David Steel is a Scotsman and a son of the manse, but because the latest opinion polls show that support for the Alliance among the elderly is leaping ahead.

I am very suspicious of opinion polls. Often they are silly, frequently they are misleading, and sometimes they are a menace.

They are silly because they ask daft questions. Would you, asked one recently, welcome advertising on BBC television if there were no decline in the standard of programmes – a question which begs the question.

They are misleading because they encourage the assumption that a count of empty heads randomly selected is a substitute for knowledge. Asking a thousand ill-informed people what they think about something they have never thought about is no substitute for analysis. Opinion is not evidence in itself. And most opinion polls tell you only about the opinion poll. The Don't Knows are the only ones I believe. Furthermore polls make both politicians and journalists lazy. It is so much easier to sample opinion than to investigate the truth.

But they are also a menace because they manipulate. It is one thing to take the temperature of the electorate between elections, quite another to sample opinion during an election campaign. Were there to be a general election tomorrow, how would you vote? is an innocent question made harmless by the very fact that there is no election tomorrow. But to ask how you are going to vote in the election a week on Thursday is to interfere with the secrecy of the ballot box. It is nobody's business but yours. Some countries forbid opinion polls during election campaigns and so should we. They set bandwaggons rolling, and they spoil the fun. I don't want to know who has won until the electorate pronounces.

None the less, asked who they would vote for now, more and more people among the over-sixties are plumping for the Alliance.

Why?

Now I don't want to get involved here in an argument about the relative merits of the political parties, their policies, or their people. But I am intrigued by this shift in the opinions of the elderly.

It is always said that the natural progression of mankind is from left to right. Youth, believing itself immortal, wants to change the world. Age, knowing itself mortal, is content to make the best of this world. Bernard Shaw, you will remember, put it more fiercely when he said that every man over forty was a scoundrel.

But perhaps there are three stages in political mankind. The young want to change the world; the middle-aged to cope with it; the elderly to understand it.

Better centuries than ours ascribed wisdom not to the busy and the successful but to the contemplative – the ancients. The very word sage means the wisdom of experience. Wisdom requires not just a past, a lifetime of experience, but the analysis of that past – the very thing opinion polls ignore.

Every wise old man or woman is a historian, because history is not the past, it is what we make of the past. Those who have lived for sixty years or more and who contemplate that experience are beyond the reach of those who simply peddle slogans. They have heard it all before.

They say that history does not repeat itself. But it does. The actors change but the lines remain the same. And the consequences.

Any political party which seeks to woo the elderly will have to do much more than promise pension increases and annual bonuses. It will have to respect their opinions.

The old are more than a lobby. They are a constituency, a growing constituency. Not all are wise, but they have the experience from which to distil wisdom.

If they choose.

Spring 1985

A Crisis of Identity
by HCDB 81/3

I can never remember my National Insurance Number. But then, who can? I can never remember my passport number either, nor my Access number. But then I seldom glance at the first except to fill in immigration forms on aeroplanes, and the second is so long that only a computer could remember it. And to be honest the reason I cannot remember any of them is because I don't want to. I know where to find them when I need them.

But I have never forgotten, nor ever will, my Identity Card number. It is HCDB 81/3. Me. I could look it up as well because it now adorns my Medical Card but I do not need to look it up because the number is engraved on my memory.

I can even remember the night I was given it. It was in the autumn of 1939, soon after war broke out. I was an evacuee in a farm in the grounds of a castle in Cumberland. A young insurance salesman, dressed like an advertisement for De Reske Minor cigarettes, called at the farm in a state of nervous excitement. He had been chosen to issue the cards. The children of the farmer and his wife had long since left home – the boys as hired hands, the girls into service. So the farmer was HCDB 81/1, his wife HCDB 81/2, and I at the age of nine became HCDB 81/3.

All that week, I remember, in the village school we called ourselves by our National Identity Numbers until the teacher said enough was enough. After that my mind is blank. I don't remember ever being asked to produce the card to prove my identity but then the Germans didn't invade and our secret plan at Great Corby School to found a junior resistance force was never put into effect.

The formal surrender of Identity Cards at the end of the war was welcomed as part of the liberation, and any suggestion of restoring them has always been thought to smack of a police state. And yet there is an argument for having them, not least to make life easier for the elderly.

Indeed some retired people are already issued with them. Those people whose pensions are paid into the bank and who do not have a pension book are given a card to attest their pensioners' rights. And it is now being suggested that pensioners should all have the right to such a card to spare them always having to carry their pension books as testimony of their claims to concessions.

One very sensible suggestion is that the card could simply be a slip attached to the pension book, which could be filled in, stamped at the Post Office, and then detached and used separately. No one could possibly jib at that. It would be like a membership card of a discount club, and no one would be compelled to carry it. As long as the card is for the convenience of the pensioner and not for the convenience of the State no one need feel got at.

Some people have gone further and suggested that there should be a pensioner's passport valid within all the countries of the EEC. Though if the EEC were to live up to its principles all EEC citizens should be free to move from one country to another within the Community without any form of passport. But that will not happen.

States are suspicious of each other's nationals. It is when a state is suspicious of its own people that we have to be wary.

The price of liberty, they say, is eternal vigilance. What the man actually said, and his name was John Philpot Curran, was this: 'The conditions upon which God hath given liberty to man is eternal vigilance.' He said it in Dublin in July, 1790, in a speech in favour of the election of Lord Mayors. Two years later they were chopping off the heads of the unelected in France in pursuit of Liberty. They spelled it with a capital L because it was an ideal, all or nothing. And before long they were chopping off the heads of those who failed to see the beauty of their argument.

That is not our way. We chopped off a king's head when he got above himself, but in this country it has been the tradition to talk not of Liberty, an ideal, but of liberties, a possession. We have our liberties and we surrender them reluctantly to the State.

English Common Law is based largely upon the assumption that you can do what you like until your behaviour so irritates your neighbours that they pass a law to regulate it. Similarly if enough of us think that something which is not being done ought to be done we urge the State on our behalf to do it. It is a helpful arrangement but it is no more than that. It does not bestow rights upon the State. Nor should it.

When the State gets above itself we expect voices to be raised in Parliament to bring it down to size. And sometimes Parliament has to be prompted by public opinion. Because if history has taught us anything it has taught us that power corrupts, that those in authority, frustrated by circumstances, will bend the rules in their own favour unless checked. That is one reason why the electorate in its wisdom switches its vote from one party to another. We also know from experience that bureaucracy would have us all tied up if we did not insist on its accountability to Parliament.

And every now and then something happens which reminds us of the need to remain alert, and not to nod off. The television programme about telephone tapping which was broadcast, after some delay, shortly before Easter was such a reminder. It is one thing to tap the phone of a man who is planning to blow up Harrods. It is quite another to tap the phone of a man who is hoping to demolish the argument for nuclear deterrence. One is a terrorist, the other a citizen of a free country seeking to exercise his right of free speech.

There is always the temptation to dismiss such allegations with a cynical joke. If your phone is tapped do you get a bit off the bill for a shared line? – that kind of crack. I often fall into that kind of temptation myself being of the opinion that governments of all persuasions are chiefly characterised by muddle and incompetence.

Things are never what they expected. When Harold Macmillan was asked what had surprised him most in all his time as prime minister, he replied: 'Events.' What matters is that events should not be made the excuse for tampering with our liberties.

Summer 1985

12

It is not
Too Much to Ask

On the day the Government published its Green Paper on the reform of social security I went in search of any relevant minister who was prepared to answer this simple question.

Who will be worse off and by how much?

But they were not letting on. Too soon, too soon, they chorused, figures will come later.

It was an answer which served only to heighten my suspicion that the poor would bear the brunt of any cost cutting, and since half the poor in Britain are pensioners, it would be many pensioners who would be worse off.

Age Concern, which knows a great deal more about this subject than I do, leapt to the same conclusion. It was pretty certain that pensioners would be the victims of any cuts. It rushed out a statement saying that pensioners were 'the sacrificial lambs at the altar of the cost cutting exercise'.

It feared, for instance, that the proposed cuts in housing benefit would affect nearly 4½ million pensioners and would intensify the tax-benefit poverty trap for those who had tried to save for their retirement.

And that was not on. Today's pensioners, it said, must be protected against cuts of any kind. Their pension is too low as it is and what they need is a major increase in their income now.

And Age Concern did not shy away from the figures.

The retirement pension, it said, should be at least a third of average earnings for a single person, which is £56, and at least half of average earnings for a couple, which is £84.

Age Concern issued that statement on the Monday. On the Thursday of the same week, having had time to examine the Green Paper more carefully and to make a calculation or two, it came out with a second statement. This one was even more adamant. It did not say that the proposals in the Green Paper *might* lead to cuts for pensioners, it said it *would* lead to cuts.

The Green Paper, it said, gave only 'promises, promises' for future pensioners, and 'substantial income cuts' for pensioners now.

Those receiving housing benefit would receive less. Those receiving supplementary benefit – the poorest of pensioners – would receive less. And as for the abolition of the death grant, that was 'cruel and insensitive'.

Age Concern was right, and what is more was right to make such a fuss, and in such a manner.

There is always a danger that any public debate about the future of the Welfare State flounders between large numbers and small stories, with one lot bandying figures in billions and the other lot swopping anecdotes.

What matters is who receives how much. And is it enough to live on?

The old age pension is too small, it is not by itself enough to live on and where it is a person's sole income it has to be supplemented.

Were it to be raised to the figures Age Concern proposes it would at least enable most pensioners to live on their pensions, albeit at subsistence level, and would spare them and the State all the hassle of claiming a multiplicity of supplementary benefits.

Anything that simplifies the system without making people worse off is to be welcomed. Nearly a million pensioners at present fail to claim money to which they are entitled simply because the system is so complicated.

And the money they forfeit could make all the difference between privation and the provision of the legitimate comforts of old age.

The social security system is in need of reform. There have been so many increases and so many amendments since Beveridge first drew up his plan that tinkering with the system will not be enough to improve it.

The methods both of collecting the money and of distributing the money need to be revised. It probably is time to discard the principle of the flat-rate contribution. Lloyd George didn't think

14

much of it in 1911 and the Chancellor made the first move to change it in his last budget.

All changes will, of course, be resisted, especially those which transfer a benefit from the rich to the poor, because the rich have more powerful voices in the land.

Politicians of all persuasions shrink from supporting the abolition of tax relief on mortage repayments even though that subsidy far exceeds the subsidy on council housing.

But necessary and overdue reforms can be accomplished if we keep a firm eye on the main purpose, which is to provide social security, and if we remember that to reform the system means 'to make it better'.

But can we afford it?

Yes, if we want to.

When politicians say 'we cannot spend taxpayers' money on this or that, what they mean is that they will not spend the money on this or that. It is a matter of political choice. Thousands of millions of pounds of taxpayers' money is spent every day with never a question asked.

And there is no better use of taxes than to provide for those in need. It is a noble purpose. You have only to visit a country where it has yet to be attempted and where poverty greets you on the pavements to be reminded of its virtue.

Of course there are those who abuse the system. But many more people fail to get benefits to which they are entitled than claim the benefits to which they are not entitled. And the old especially should not be short-changed.

It is not much to ask of a developed nation that its inhabitants should end their days in decent comfort. At the height of the Second World War it was thought to be the very least that the nation could do for its people. Hence the Beveridge Plan.

Twenty years later and twenty years ago, A. J. P. Taylor, in his book *English History 1914–1945*, wrote this of the Beveridge Plan:

'It came some forty years too late and provided, as might be expected, against past evils: abject poverty and mass unemployment, one the great social evil before 1914, and the other between the Wars. Neither was to present a problem after 1945.'

Would that that were so.

Abject poverty is perhaps a thing of the past although there are still far too many people in this country living on or below the poverty line, not least among the elderly.

But mass unemployment is with us again and shows little sign of abating.

So we still need the kind of social security system which Beveridge devised, with its contributions and its benefits.

And we need to make a better fist of it.

Autumn 1985

My Uncle and the Inner City

My favourite uncle has died, he was almost as old as the century. He worked in the Town Hall for forty years, lived in the same house for fifty years, and sang in the Cathedral choir for sixty years. He was not a rich man, indeed he was a man of very modest means, but he lived a very rich life.

He lived in a terraced house on the edge of the inner city and was much amused that his annual rates bill was latterly more than the original purchase price of the house. He had walked to work every day of his working life, never owned and never had any need of a car. But then he was not acquisitive. He had his prized possessions – a piano which he played every day, some excellent oil paintings which hung on his walls for half a century to my knowledge – but he coveted nothing.

He knew that it is not what a man possesses but what he is and what he does that makes for fulfillment, and he was very fulfilled. His pastimes were not mere hobbies to be discarded with each passing fancy, but essential parts of his life – his singing, his worship, his conduct of the local chamber music society, the oldest in Britain. He never missed an important cultural event in the city, and he went not to fill up his diary or to be seen to be there but because that was all part of civilised living.

He was urban man, not suburban man. He liked the countryside. He would put on stout shoes, take a stout stick, get on a train into the country and walk many a mile. But he was above all a city dweller. He looked upon the city as an arena for his enjoyment. He knew every inch of it and had only pity for those who would diminish its activities.

He was pretty set in his ways, but he was not reactionary. I had lunch with him to celebrate what was to be his last birthday on this earth and he explained to me with much merriment why the Bishop of Durham was right and his critics wrong. He is not saying anything, he said, that Paul didn't say.

His life was never frantic, anxious, disorganised, or empty. He never sat slumped in front of the television because he had nothing else to do. He started the day with a proper breakfast and had no time for the continental alternative. He could not, he said, understand how grown men could eat bread and jam for breakfast every day of their lives. Properly fortified he would set off for work with ample time to spare, greeting those he strode past on the street, and if he was in the mood singing a favourite aria.

He never moaned about his own comparatively lowly task and took great delight in observing the antics and the anxieties of his masters. He was a great observer of the human scene and his enthusiasms were boundless. And when he was wrong headed, as he sometimes was, he was the first to mock himself. The seasons of the church governed his years, the calendar of the city his activities.

His retirement was not the onset of an exile. He did not disappear into a suburban enclave or a seaside estate. He lived where he had always lived, walked the same streets, frequented the same places of assembly, attended the same place of worship. If anything his life was even fuller.

Of course he was lucky. His pension though small was secure, his health until the last years robust. But then, as I said, he never hankered for possessions he could not afford, and his daily regimen was healthy in itself. His inner life was tranquil, his public life absorbing. In short, I think he understood the secret of a happy life. Certainly his pensioned years were what I would wish for everyone's pensioned years – sufficient means and ample appetite for living.

His death set me wondering whether we are making it too difficult to lead an urban life. First there were all those wrong planning decisions – the wholesale clearances, the high-rise developments, the overspill, the multi-storey this and that. Then all that redevelopment to make the city a place for the motorist, for the shopper, for the credit card carrier but not really for the inhabitants.

It has produced an alienation so that those who can afford it can't wait to get out and those remaining are too often the poor and the deprived. But cities are not supposed to be places like that, locked up at night when it is unsafe to be out. The city is where people should come together not just to work but for all their communal activities. The inner city is where the action should be.

The ancient Greeks knew that. And so did my favourite uncle.

Winter 1985

Here Beginneth
the Lesson of 1986

Nineteen-eighty-six is Industry Year in Britain.
So what, you may think, every year is industry year in Britain and has been since 1786 or even earlier. We are an industrial nation, the first industrial nation, and the evidence is all about us. Monuments to past industrial achievements decorate the landscape and rarely a week goes by without someone somewhere opening yet another museum to commemorate our industrial heritage.

But that is our trouble. We have a more successful industrial past than present, and the future is very uncertain. For the truth is that the first industrial nation in the world has become an also-ran, and 1986 is the year in which we shall have to ask ourselves what has gone wrong and, far more important, what we are going to do about it. Because, let us not pretend, without industry we are nothing.

No one who faces the facts can deny that we have fallen behind. Our declining performance as a manufacturing nation is masked by the income we now get from oil. But the oil will not last for ever, and the fear is that when it is used up we shall have neither the manufacturing capacity nor the skilled workforce to replace the income lost. Already we import more manufactured goods than we export.

Why?

There is no shortage of explanations because everybody blames everybody else. The trade unions are told that it is all their fault because they are opposed to change or put too high a price on it. Management is told that it is to blame for being afraid of change and for always playing safe, as if promotion to a top job was a reward rather than a challenge. The money-lenders in the City of London are accused of failing to invest in change, of not supporting new manufacturing ventures, preferring instead to make their fortunes in easier speculation.

Successive governments, who take it very personally when criticised, are accused of rushing hastily into ill-considered change. And the education system is blamed for having little or no interest in industry, changed or unchanged.

There is truth in all those accusations but they are the symptoms not the cause, of Britain's industrial decline. The truth goes back much further and extends much farther. A hundred years ago there were those who feared that Britain was slipping behind, and as early as 1841 George Stephenson was complaining about the shortage of trained engineers.

It was precisely because we were the first industrial nation that we got set in our ways. We did it first so we assumed not only that we did it best, but that there was no other way to do it. Custom and practice were the watchwords in British Industry and the Empire was our tame market. But other people were doing things differently and doing them better, and we scarcely seemed to notice. Industry had given us an Empire and made this country for a while the most powerful nation on earth. But we took the rewards while disparaging the means.

And that, it seems to me, is the real cause of Britain's industrial decline. For those in high places industry was something neither to be seen nor heard. Robert Peel's grandfather, Old Parsley Peel, a calico printer who said you could have any pattern on your print provided it was parsley, was happy to live within sight of the mill in Rossendale. His grandson looked for the life of the country gentleman and the Westminster politician.

Industry was not a calling for a gentleman. In Victorian England it was thought better to be a landowner, a member of a profession, a clergyman, an officer of the Crown, but not – pray not – an industrialist. That was vulgar. We even devised an education system – the public school system – which not only chose to ignore industry, but took great pains to steer its ablest pupils well away from industry. Sociologists call this cultural disparagement: I call it snobbery. What is certain is that it is the reason Britain has fallen behind as an industrial nation. We simply do not take industry seriously.

And yet we cannot do without it. It is not true that we can

21

slide gracefully into a post-industrial society (whatever that is) with everyone growing his own clothes and dancing round the Maypole to entertain the tourists. Not with our population, not with our expectation.

We expect there to be a place in school for every child, a bed in hospital for every patient, a job for every citizen. And already we are having difficulty achieving that. Not to mention that we expect all the adornments of civilised living – private comfort and public splendour. We expect the streets to be swept, the buses to run, the shops to open, the theatres to perform.

Nor is it true, as some of our dafter politicians suggest, that the days of manufacturing are over. People want more and more things – a car each, and all the gadgetry of home entertainment and telecommunications. The Japanese have grown rich supplying Britain with video recorders. It is only the methods of manufacture that change.

And that is precisely what we must be doing – applying the new technology to making of things. It is not as if we know not how. The first computer in the world was built in Britain, and we are a most ingenious people. A Japanese research team recently looked for the origin of the hundred most successful post-war industries. They discovered that the ideas for 55 per cent of them came from Britain. We just had not bothered to do much about them.

So what are we going to do? Or, more accurately, what *must* we do if we are not to fall further and further behind? The answer is very simple:

We must take it seriously.

We must recognise as a nation that industry is the most important activity in our national life. Where else can the money come from.

I believe that most ordinary people know that. It is the first lesson that life teaches them. But it is at the top that the lesson will now have to be learned. The great and the good who assume or achieve pre-eminence in our country (and who reward themselves twice a year in the Honours List) will have to recapture the industrial spirit. They will have to cure themselves of the arch mock modesty of failing to understand the new technology and all its implications. It is beyond me, they say winsomely, meaning that they think it is beneath them.

The education system will have to make sure that no one can emerge from it ignorant of the importance of industry or of what must happen in industry. We already have a situation where the young who have mastered the computer at junior school can find no one to teach them advanced mathematics in senior school.

In industry itself we shall have to make a better job of work, and that means that we shall have to make a better use of people. The same technology is now available throughout the world. Success in the market goes to the workforce that can use the technology to the best advantage. The workforce has to be not only competent in using the technology, but also eager to learn, ready to change, and determined to produce the best quality product.

You cannot achieve any of that by ordering people about or by drawing up battlefields in the workplace. When *them* and *us* are at daggers drawn, the customer is forgotten and the competitor thrives. We have to go about industry in a far more intelligent way, not telling people what to do but explaining what needs to be done, and letting them work out the best way. It already happens in the best British companies, where they have briefing groups and quality circles and new working agreements and full involvement. But it is the exception here and the norm in many other countries.

So if the nation wants to get its hands on the wealth that industry alone can create, it too must shed its ignorance and its prejudices. It must learn to value industry and those who work in it.

That should be the lesson of 1986 and ever after.

January 1986

Seeing the Woods
for the Trees

Nine hundred years ago they counted all the trees in this country and they published their findings in the Domesday Book.

If they had repeated the count once every hundred years thereafter it would not have changed all that much over several centuries. But if they were to do it now they would not need a book, they could jot down the figure on the back of an envelope.

Since the Second World War, we (or rather they – because it probably was not you and it certainly was not me) *they* have destroyed half the broad-leafed woodland in Britain.

Yes, half.

I first learned about this threat to our native woodland five years ago when I interviewed John James, the director of the Woodland Trust, on the 'Today' programme one morning. I had not until then heard of the Woodland Trust but I was so persuaded by what he had to say that when he asked me if I would make a Radio Appeal for the Trust I agreed at once.

At ten to nine one Sunday morning on Radio 4 I held forth with great enthusiasm on the work of the Trust. Whole woods and spinneys of oak and ash and beech are disappearing under the bulldozer and the plough, I said, and it has to stop. A landscape without trees is about as inviting as the surface of the moon.

Something has to be done and something is being done, I said, by the Woodland Trust. The Trust has two simple aims: to protect trees, and to plant trees. It buys up woodland, and at that time had acquired fifty woods in fourteen counties.

The public response to the Appeal was overwhelming. People clearly feel very strongly about trees and care deeply about woodland. Not only did they give generously but they enrolled by the hundred as members of the Woodland Trust.

Two years later I broadcast a second Appeal. I was able to report that every penny they had donated had been used to buy woods. It now owned nearly a hundred woods in twenty-seven counties. And its membership over the two years had risen from ten thousand to twenty-five thousand. It was acquiring another wood every month.

This time the response was even greater. Twice as much money poured in; twice as many people clamoured to join. So last year, when I made a television appeal for the Trust, I was able to report that it now had four hundred thousand members and was looking after one hundred and thirty woods in thirty counties of England and Wales, and had just purchased its first wood in Scotland.

It had also just bought a wood in Dorset which contains a mighty pollarded lime tree which is certainly the oldest living thing in the county and possibly the oldest living thing in England. It was there when they did the Domesday count and the wood was then valued at £9. It came on the market last year at £100,000, and there was no shortage of developers anxious to buy it and chop it down for development, but the Trust raised the money to buy it and the wood is now safe for generations to come.

And that is the whole purpose of the exercise.

If things were allowed to go on as they have been, all – and I mean all – our most valuable woods outside the nature reserves – all the ones which delight the eye and shelter the wildlife – would have disappeared by the end of the century. And the end of the century is only fourteen years away.

The matter is as urgent as that.

Did you know that if all the hedgerows in Britain which have been torn down since 1945 were to be laid end to end, they would stretch six times round the world?

To protest is not enough. Words alone will not halt the desecration. If there is money to be made, the hedgerows will be torn out and the trees will be felled. Ownership is the only protection.

A member of the Trust in Hertfordshire alerted it to the sale of Wormley Wood, 350 acres of rare oak and hornbeam. They were chopping it down to plant conifers in boring rows. So the Trust bought it – a very big purchase – and Wormley Wood is now secure.

And when I say secure I don't mean cordoned off, preserved but unvisited. All the woods the Woodland Trust looks after are open for everyone to enjoy. That is the point of a wood, something to look at and wander through. 'Let us go for a walk in the woods' have been welcome words for centuries.

And when I say that the woods are open for everyone to enjoy, I include the wildlife. This, after all, is their home, always has been and always should be.

We do not want a world without woods or woodland, without food or shelter for wildlife, and without natural pleasures for people. We have more than enough concrete, more than enough sodium light, more than enough noise.

We want to be sure that a hundred years from now, and a thousand years from now, there will still be broad-leafed woodland in Britain.

We owe it to posterity.

March 1986

Nap on Cats

Nineteen-eighty-six is, among other things, the Year of the Cat. It is the year in which cat lovers have got together to make sure that their favourite creature is no longer the underdog. Supporters of the Year of the Cat are eager to promote cats as companions for the elderly.

Age Concern has gone further. It has put PEP into 1986. PEP is the Pets and Elderly People Campaign, a campaign to draw attention to the importance of pets (all pets – animals and birds and fishes) as living companions to old people. Age Concern is administering the PEP Campaign and many other organisations have joined in.

I should hope so too. I have long believed that everyone should have a pet at every age – a white mouse when you are little, a black cat when you are old.

At one time my children went in for Peruvian guinea pigs, which may explain why my eldest son subsequently went off to Peru to count monkeys for a living. And we have always had cats.

At the moment we have five. The eldest is Scoobie, universally known as Faithful Scoob. He is old and grey and a bit rheumaticky, and whoever rings up always asks after him first.

Leo is almost as old. He is long-haired and handsome. Eight years ago some cruel unthinking person locked him in a garage and he was found three weeks later, reduced to skin and bone. The RSPCA asked us to take him in and he soon settled and throve.

Lilah is female, tortoiseshell, and difficult. She used to be Delilah and had a brother called Samson, an incorrigible cat who sadly was run over.

Oscar and Emmy, the latest members of the family, are little Cockney cats. They were born in the cellar of a Town Hall in London and rescued by CAT, the Cat Action Trust, a charity of which I am proud to be President.

CAT exists to solve the problem of the feral cat. Feral cats are domestic cats living wild, either because they have strayed from home or more commonly because they are unwanted and have been expelled from home, thrown out.

Feral cats do not walk alone. They gather in colonies wherever they can find food and shelter – in backyards, on building sites, in hospital gardens, in every urban corner. They are the inhabitants of dereliction.

And they multiply. A healthy female can give birth to 120 kittens in her single lifetime. So if nothing is done to control the population of a feral colony, the cats soon over-run the neighbourhood and the neighbours object.

Enter the Cat Action Trust.

Its volunteer workers visit the cat colonies, trap the cats, and take them to the vet to be spayed or neutered. Then they return the adult cats (who are too old to mend their feral ways) to the sites and organise feeding rotas.

And they find good homes for the kittens, which is how we came to get Oscar and Emmy. They arrived on Good Friday last year, aged six weeks, having travelled in a basket from London to Cheshire. They stepped out of the basket without a moment's hesitation, marched into the house – to the surprise of the other three – and made themselves at home.

They are now huge. Emmy is black and white, has a pink nose, and talks non-stop. Oscar is nearly all black, looks like a rug on the move, rummages all night in the hedgerows, and is known as That Cat.

We would not be without any of them.

Pets are good for you, and they are especially good for the elderly, as an increasing amount of research is revealing.

Dorothy Walster of the Scottish Health Education Group published a report two or three years ago in which she set out to discover what the companionship of an animal can do not only to improve the quality of life of old people but also to prevent the onset of ill-health and the worsening of chronic conditions.

She gathered evidence from all over the place about the value of companion animals to older people as comforters and friends. Her analysis of the material suggested that pet ownership makes a strong contribution to health in body and mind.

And she concluded that in these days of increasing reliance on community care 'an alternative therapy to conventional medical practice can be found in pet ownership.'

Animals, she said, are companions twenty-four hours of the day and ask little in return for the benefits they bestow on their owners. Responsible pet ownership removes fears of loneliness, and animals may be spoken to without fear of being thought 'odd' or answering back.

She even made a list of common problems usually alleviated by taking the tablets or waiting for the social worker, and suggested how a pet might help instead.

People who are apathetic have something to care for.

People who are bereaved have a link with the lost person.

People who are confused have an animal's timetable to attend to.

People who are depressed have something to think about.

People who are cold have something warm to cuddle.

People who are immobile have somethig to stroke.

People who are lonely have someone to talk to.

And people who are suicidal have a reason to live.

The truth is that people with pets live longer because they know that they are needed. Animals offer love and reassurance without criticism, and stimulate our natural tendency to offer support and protection.

If you don't believe me, ask our cats.

June 1986

An Annexe
to Heaven

'This place,' said the rigger, a tattooed man not given to gentle utterances, 'is like an annexe to heaven.'

This place was a hospice, a home for the terminally ill, to which I had taken a television crew in order to film an appeal. The crew had been reluctant to go, afraid they readily confessed of coming face to face with the dying.

But once inside their fears vanished and they found themselves in warm and eager conversation with the patients as well as the staff. The peace which permeates a hospice embraced them too.

I have seen it happen to so many people. A group of teenagers looking for somewhere to sing carols on a Christmas Eve asked my advice and I persuaded them to visit the local hospice. They went in trepidation, and emerged in quiet triumph. It had been, they said, one of the most rewarding experiences of their young lives.

The hospice movement, I think, is the best thing that has happened in this country since the Second World War.

Thirty years ago there were no beds, no facilities, no nursing or medical staff anywhere in Britain concerned wholly and solely with the care of those who were incurably ill.

Then as now, when you took ill and your illness was diagnosed, doctors classified you as a particular case – medical, surgical, obstetric, whatever – so that you might be given the appropriate treatment and with luck cured.

But if you could be neither classified nor cured, if you were incurably ill, then the health service could do no more for you. Death was your business not theirs, and indeed they, and society as a whole, were reluctant to talk about it. It was like a confession of failure.

But today, thanks to the tireless efforts of some inspired individuals and some energetic charities, there are getting on for a hundred special nursing units in the country whose sole function is to care for the terminally ill.

These are the hospices.

Of course their own homes are the first choice of those who are incurably ill, among their nearest and dearest, and Home Care nursing teams based on the local hospice visit patients at home both to help with the nursing and to advise the family.

They understand that the immediate family of a patient who is incurably ill are in a sense patients too, in need of help to cope with the pain and the stress.

And when the pain and the distress become too much both for the patient and for the family the Home Care staff arrange for the patient to be transferred to the hospice.

Need is the only criterion for entry. It is not a matter of who you are or what you are but only of how ill you are. Hospice patients can be both in-patients and out-patients and a hospice combines the freedom of home with the complete care of the patient and support for the family.

Hospice care is much more than the provision of clean sheets and cool hands. It is a combination of staff, services, and the community – all dedicated to the tender and loving care of the patients.

Every patient is met at the door of a hospice, welcomed, made to feel immediately at home. The medical, nursing, and ancillary staff are not only dedicated and highly trained, but profoundly aware of the needs of incurably ill people.

The nurse:patient ratio is usually one to one.

A patient has only to raise a whisper for there to be a nurse at the bedside, talking, listening, comforting.

This communion of nurse and patient is the very heart of the work of the hospice. It is real nursing – the care of one human being by another, not just the dispensation of treatment.

Medically the hospice is concerned above all to remove both pain and the expectation of pain, to restore to the patient both comfort and dignity.

Pain-killing drugs are often served in a drink and as the pain dissolves and the fear of its return is lessened, so the dependence on drugs decreases and the patients are more themselves.

Visiting hours are virtually unlimited. Relatives, friends, children, even pets, are welcomed at almost any hour.

There are toys for the children to play with, quiet rooms where older relatives can chat undisturbed, a communal lounge for those who want to be sociable. And if the need arises close relatives can usually stay overnight.

And anything that any patient wants to do is encouraged. Because a hospice is not simply a place for the care of the dying. It is a testament to the joy of living.

Its inspiration is religious. It affirms that life is not simply chronological, a matter of how long each of us can live, but theological, and concerned with the pursuit of the perfection of the moment.

Patients in hospices, staff in hospices, voluntary helpers in hospices – all find themselves understanding this truth. A hospice is a holy place, or, as the rigger said, an annexe to heaven.

July 1986

The Difficulty
of Finding
Good Servants

Throughout Lent this year BBC Radio posed the question:
What on earth is the Church for? No clear answer emerged.
It was not, it appeared, the question people wanted to be asked.

Instead, in a series of phone-ins on local radio and in a final
huge discussion on Radio 4, contributor after contributor from
parish groups all over the country rushed to say what the Church
was not.

It was not, they said, just the clergy. This was a curious denial
because no one had suggested that it was. And no one in his
right mind would claim that ministry in the Church can be
limited to those who are ordained.

For good or ill everyone serves the believing community they
belong to, whether they want to or not. They do this by the
honesty of their doubt as well as by the strength of their faith.
But they can damage the message they have been given by the
dishonesty of prejudice or by the ignorance of bigotry.

Everyone who is a Christian is a minister or servant and it is
good that there is a move back to the old idea of a multiplication
of ministries. BUT, and it is a very big BUT, these ministries
must be used to bolster and not to obscure the power of the
Gospel message.

I was in Downing Street, of all places, with a TV crew recently
and the director, a born-again Christian of recent conversion,
solemnly assured me that the sun was shining on our endeavours
because he had prayed for it the night before.

'It always happens for me now,' he said. I have known him
since long before he took leave of his senses, so I pointed out
very firmly that such a foolish utterance was superstition not
religion. He was suitably abashed.

Even vicars can succumb to such folly. In the parish next to mine the Vicar chose recently to adorn his church with a poster which read: 'Jesus reaches the parts that even Heineken doesn't reach.' I hope that someone pointed out to him that even an excess of evangelicalism does not excuse such silliness.

The sign of the priestly ministry is very important, not least to those outside the Church. It can be the excuse for the rejection of faith or the first invitation to it.

I think that the Gospel message is one that people want to hear but that they will only listen if it is expressed in a clear language which can encompass life and death, and admit mystery.

I think that priests should not be afraid of holiness. They should not be self-conscious about their priesthood. As a friend of mine is fond of saying, it is nothing personal. In the upside-down hierarchy of Calvary it places them firmly at the bottom with only the bishops to break their fall.

I don't want them to be like stage vicars, ineffectually genteel, like a cross between a maiden aunt and a hamster.

I don't want to hear them talk in the jargon of sociology or psychotherapy. In the Bible, the more difficult the idea, the simpler the language. Look at the beginning of St John.

I want them to preach the Gospel because I believe the Christian story is not so much rejected as not known.

I want them to be theological and to challenge the dottier ideas of the fundamentalists.

I want them to take a Christian view of politics and not be afraid to speak out.

I want them to ask more of people. The whole point of a pilgrimage is not the distance covered but the act of identifying yourself with a purpose larger than your own.

Christianity is not just a matter of Sunday observance. It is not enough to pray only in church and only when the vicar is looking.

The story is told that when Mao Tse-Tung was on his deathbed, someone read to him The Sermon on the Mount. When the reading finished Mao said: 'It is just as well the Christians only read it and do not act upon it, otherwise there would be no need for my little Red Book.'

The truth is that priests have in their giving a gift greater than any other. They must believe that, and yet they are often seen to appear to withold it through an excess of good manners.

I said all this and much more recently at a conference attended by all the clergy of a single diocese. To my surprise they took it very well. The questions I was raising were questions they ask themselves.

But one or two who were present were offended, and said so. And in the subsequent debate I discovered that they were the prisoners of a brittle and unbending belief.

Like my friend, the TV director in Downing Street, they were looking for certainty and immediate reward.

But the Church has a greater mission.

September 1986

A Winter's Tale

On the morning after the coldest night of last winter I landed in a helicopter on a snow-covered hill high above Merthyr Tydfil in the Welsh Valleys. I was there to make a video programme.

The cameraman, unfortuntely, had forgotten the camera so we had to fly to Cardiff to get another, but eventually, two hours late, I held forth to a borrowed camera on top of that hill.

I talked about fuel poverty, about the inability of people, especially old people, to keep warm at a price they can afford. Faced with a choice between eating or heating because they cannot afford both, some eat and freeze, others heat and starve.

Recent research has revealed that what old people most fear is the indignity of debt, so they will not run up fuel bills that they cannot pay. They would rather go hungry, or shiver. Or sit all day in the public library. And so every winter the headlines recite a toll of death from hypothermia or malnutrition.

Why does this happen?

The simple answer is: because too many old people do not have enough money. But I suspect it will be a very long time before the nation provides an adequate old age pension for everyone.

The second reason is the price of fuel. In the last ten years the price of electricity, for instance, has gone up by more than 500 per cent, but the retail price index upon which State benefits are based has gone up by less than 400 per cent. And it is no secret that the index underestimates the increase in the cost of living of the poor.

But there is a third reason and it is this: Britain has the coldest homes in Europe. In spite of the high cost of fuel we allow most of the heat to escape.

Denmark and Britain have much the same climate, and in summer the death rate in the two countries is about the same. In winter, when the outside temperatures are little different, the death rate in Britain is more than twice that in Denmark.

Quite literally old people here freeze to death. The cause of death is not always diagnosed as hypothermia, for pneumonia more likely will have set in first, or heart failure, but the common cause is the cold.

It is estimated that seventy-seven thousand people die in Britain every winter not because of the climate outside but because of the climate inside. Their homes are freezing. Half the old people in this country come down every winter morning into a living room too cold for health or comfort.

So what can be done?

The answer is very simple. Stop the cold getting in and the heat getting out. Make every house draught-proof and insulated. That will make the houses warmer and the heating bills smaller.

Every DIY store stocks the necessary materials – draught excluders, loft insulation, hot water tank jackets. Local councils can provide grants towards the cost of the first two and when people are on supplementary benefit the DHSS will pay for a hot water tank jacket.

BUT . . . the sad fact is that many elderly people neither know that these materials are readily available, nor that grants may be available to help pay for them. And in any case they may be too old to shin up ladders to get into the loft. Which is why I came to be standing on that snow-covered hill above Merthyr Tydfil.

The video programme we were making was for Neighbourhood Energy Action, a charity based in Newcastle-upon-Tyne, whose purpose is to encourage, in co-operation with the Department of Energy and the Manpower Services Commission, neighbourhood energy projects.

Already the Charity has set in motion projects all over the kingdom, from the North of Scotland to the Channel coast. Nearly three hundred projects so far, with new ones starting every month.

Two hundred thousand houses – the homes of old people and

poor people – are warmer now, draught-proofed and insulated, as a result of the work of a neighbourhood energy project.

Merthyr Tydfil is a good example of how they go about their good work. They set up a team. First a surveyor to visit people in their cold homes, to work out precisely what needs to be done, to fill in the forms, to reassure the old people that this is a community exercise not a commercial venture.

Then a group of skilled tradesmen to do the work in the house – the draught-proofing, the loft insulation, the pipe-lagging, whatever. And in Merthyr they insist on using the best materials available.

They also take care not to over-do it. They make certain that there is enough ventilation for the safe operation of gas heaters and open fires. And they have energy advisers to make sure that the old people use fuel wisely and get the most for their money.

I saw the results for myself, not by knocking at doors and asking to go in, but from above, from the helicopter looking down on the roof tops.

The houses with snow on their roofs were the warm houses. The snow melts first on the roofs of the houses where the heat is being allowed to escape.

There is, it seems to me, no more urgent task than to make sure that the old are not cold in their own homes. It is not something that should be postponed. It is no good saying to someone who is getting on that he or she will be warm next winter. They should be warm this winter. Like the Danes.

November/December 1986

Five Million . . .
and One

F ive million people ride bicycles in Beijing, five million and
one when the Queen was there. I was the one. I borrowed a
bike because it seemed the best way to get about and to get to
meet the people, of whom there are many.

I have seen multitudes before, in India for instance, and
Beijing (as we must now learn to call Peking, because everybody
else does) is not unlike New Delhi. But whereas the streets of
New Delhi are filled with people of different races and religions
and preoccupations and even centuries (you can bump into
medieval man on the pavement there) in Beijing everyone seems
to belong and to belong now.

They are all one people and it is impossible not to like them.
There is no mystery. They are not inscrutable people, but open
and friendly. They looked relieved not oppressed, happy to be
alive and glad to be rid of the past. They do not press or strive
as they pedal through Beijing but bowl along through the Gate
of Heavenly Peace, or wherever, gossiping cheerfully with the
air of people for whom life, if not heavenly, is certainly better
than it was.

Beijing is not a beautiful city; the Duke of Edinburgh was
right about that. The Ming bits are beautiful – the Forbidden
City, the Temple of Heaven Park – but the bulk of it is either
Soviet brutal or workers' instant. It is however a very safe city,
in no way threatening or sinister. I saw no police with guns, no
muggers, no beggars, no dogs. Only people.

In Shanghai, which was not an imperial city but an imperialist
city, there are even more people. In Beijing no one honks a horn;
in Shanghai they do little else, and no one takes the slightest
notice. A Scottish sociologist who is teaching there told me that

there are so many people in China that everyone has only a tiny bit of social space each, so they treasure it and ignore the turmoil around them.

An English student there went further. Everybody is out on the streets of Shanghai, he said, because where else can they get any privacy. It is no use a courting couple going back to his place or hers because all the family will be in one room, mother looking askance and father giggling.

Instead you see them walking the streets demurely, hand in hand, behaving as if there is no one there but them, even though there is a bus hooting an inch behind them, a car on either side trying to run over their feet, and a bicycle seeking to bisect them.

The children are even more oblivious to the traffic. There is a law in Shanghai which forbids the carriage of small children on the front of bicycles. It is totally ignored. All small children travel on the front of their parents' bicycles and there is nothing the police dare do, for a child in China is not to be contradicted.

It must be the best place in the world to be little. The Chinese have always made a great fuss of children but they spoil them even more now that there are so few of them – only a few hundred million.

The population has grown so big that a married couple is allowed to have only one child, though I did see a man in Beijing who had identical twin daughters and he looked very smug. But imagine a nation of only children, and I speak as an only child. The little boys have the best of it. You see them in Beijing being pushed along in prams like polished orange boxes by their weary grandmothers. The boys stand upright wearing little peaked caps like soldiers – over-dressed, overfed, smirking, their every whim their grandmothers' command. Little monsters really. I am not surprised that China is beginning to have problems of delinquency among those in their early teens.

But most of the little ones are lovely. I went to a kindergarten in a textile town north of Beijing and they all sang for me. I also went into a worker's home there. In China they have show families as we have show flats, and the man of the house in this immaculate flat was the most handsome man I have ever seen in my life. No wonder they showed him off.

I got a more typical picture of family life one Sunday in Beijing when I had lunch with a family I had met by chance.

The back alleys of Beijing are filled with small houses, each built around three sides of a tiny courtyard and sealed off from the street by double doors. The family I visited once owned their whole house – all three sides of the courtyard – but now they are allowed only one side and two other families occupy the rest. It is very crowded, and the other two families have to use the public loo, for they have none of their own. And yet there was no hint of conflict or aggression.

Most people in China belong to a unit of employment – a factory or a school or a government office – which provides both a small income and a place to live. Rents are low, food is cheap, clothes too. So the bulk of the people though poor are sure of being fed and clothed and sheltered. But like people the world over they want more than that. And certainly more for their children.

The rules have therefore been relaxed following the arrest of the Gang of Four and the collapse of the Cultural Revolution. People are now allowed to earn more. The peasants work for themselves not just for the State. They are State tenants and give a proportion of their crops to the State as rent but sell the rest themselves.

The man next door to the people I lunched with has set himself up as a painter and decorator and is now rich enough to have a television set and a motor bike. When I asked if those on fixed State income were jealous, the answer was simple and direct. No, they said, we all want to be rich and someone must be rich first.

In Beijing they go to bed early, or used to. The streets were always deserted by nine o'clock. But now there are night markets open late, rows of stalls selling fast food and the latest fashions from Hong Kong, and the young flock there. The stall holders too are growing rich.

The truth is that the Chinese government wants both the country and the people to be better off. No one in China now disputes that the Cultural Revolution was a disaster, and they do not want to suffer anything like that again.

Is China, then, still a Communist country? The strict answer is, No it is not. It is run by the Chinese Communist Party but it is not and never has been a Communist country because no country has ever achieved Communism and probably never will.

41

And if the Cultural Revolution was a taste of what it would be like, no one will ever want to again.

China now, as every intellectual I talked to told me, is a Marxist country seeking to integrate Marxism with Chinese reality. They no longer say: to each according to his needs, but to each according to his labour. And egalitarianism is a dirty word.

They are not going to imitate the latest excesses of the West because they regard such antics as merger mania as silly and destructive, but no more are they going to seek to control everything. The track suit has replaced the Mao suit and the country is up and running.

The wisest white woman I met in China, a missionary's daughter, who had been imprisoned by the Japanese and insulted by the Gang of Four, but who still lives and teaches in Shanghai, said quite simply: this country is about to take off.

January/February 1987

Never a
Better Man

I do not know many people who are one hundred years old or more, and sadly I now know one fewer. Sir Harry Platt, who was born in Lancashire in 1886 and became one of the most famous orthopaedic surgeons in the world, died in Manchester just before the turn of the year.

Harry Platt was rare among great men. He liked talking about his profession, as many doctors do, but not about himself. He would tell fascinating stories about incidents and developments in which he had been involved but the heroes were always others.

He once addressed the Royal College of Surgeons on the subject of Great Men and began by confessing that he was a convinced hero-worshipper. He then talked about William Thorburn, a Manchester surgeon, who could without prompting tell the vintage year and the shipper of any glass of port placed before him, and there were many. Thorburn invited the young Platt to assist him at a private operation, and when the operation was complete, handed his young assistant a golden sovereign and a shilling. 'Your first fee,' he said.

Sir Harry also talked that day about Grafton Elliot Smith, who was Professor of Anatomy in Manchester in the early years of this century, and who once gave the young Platt a demonstration of how the brain functions by holding a fresh brain in his hand and picking it to pieces. 'It was,' said Sir Harry, 'a revelation.'

But the man he most liked to talk about was Sir Robert Jones, the founder of modern orthopaedic surgery.

Jones, who was born in Rhyl, came to Liverpool in the 1870s, to be apprenticed to his uncle, Hugh Owen Thomas, the bone-setter. The Thomas family had practised bone-setting on the isle of Anglesey for generations, and H.O. was especially skilled at making ingenious splints for the damaged children and injured dockers of Liverpool.

But Robert Jones decided that rest and fixation were not in themselves enough for the treatment of diseases of the joints, so he trained as a doctor and a surgeon, and his rooms at 11, Nelson Street, Liverpool, were soon to become world-famous.

Jones was the first surgeon to open a knee for a cartilage operation, and the first to open a hip and cover the head of a diseased femur with gold foil so that it might function again.

When Harry Platt was five years old he developed a tubercular infection of his left knee and he was taken by his father to see Robert Jones in his rooms in Nelson Street. Jones fixed the knee and cemented a friendship. When Harry grew up he decided to follow in the steps of his hero, Robert Jones.

His hero was much more than a surgeon. He was a great organiser. For five years he was consultant surgeon to the Manchester Ship Canal Company at the time when the Canal was being dug, and there he organised the first accident service in the history of British surgery.

There was a chain of first-aid stations along the thirty-five miles of the canal and three base hospitals. Each hospital – a wooden building – was staffed by a matron, two nurses, a cook, and a handyman.

A team of doctors under Jones dealt with the minor injuries and ailments of the canal workers, and severely injured patients were brought to the nearest base hospital by the overland railway which ran along the canal excavation. Jones himself was summoned by telegram to the major accident and surgical emergencies. In five years more than three thousand major accident cases were treated.

Jones, who used to run a free Sunday morning clinic in Liverpool for the very poor, went on to open the first open air orthopaedic hospital for children in Britain and then a second. And when he visited the wards the children would shout out their welcomes.

In the First World War, because of his reputation and the success of his Ship Canal accident service, Robert Jones was appointed Director of Military Orthopaedics and was eventually in charge of a group of military hospitals with more than thirty thousand beds.

And Harry Platt was with him. He had joined the man he was to call 'the greatest mender of the maimed' after graduating from Manchester University Medical School. Sir Harry was always fond of remembering the extremely elderly students who were to be found in those days wandering the corridors of the teaching hospital. Once they had paid two fees – one for the course in the theory of medicine, and one for the clinical tuition in the hospital, students could stay forever. And many did, endlessly failing and re-sitting their exams.

But not Harry. He passed with honours, and after serving with Jones in the War, and a spell of study in the States, he returned to Manchester where for twenty years at Ancoats Hospital he was friend and surgeon to the poor of the city.

In 1932 he founded the orthopaedic department at Manchester Royal Infirmary, and people came from all over the world to be treated by him. The medical students of Manchester used to chant this little verse.

> *Harry Platt, Harry Platt,*
> *You mustn't say that,*
> *You'll frighten the nurses away.*
> *Or faster and faster,*
> *They'll swathe you in plaster,*
> *Till you look like King*
> *Tutalchamay.*

He was appointed Professor of Orthopaedic Surgery in Manchester in 1939 and during the Second World War held the same commanding position as Major-General Sir Robert Jones had in the First.

Harry Platt was knighted, feted, praised. Yet a few years ago, when I had the great pleasure of interviewing him on television in Manchester about his life, he talked not about himself but about his mentor Jones and his pupil Sir John Charnley, the man who perfected the hip replacement operation.

'I was only a practitioner,' he said. 'I didn't push orthopaedics forward as Jones did and Charnley has.'

But in the next fortnight I received nothing but letters from people all over the north west of England telling me what Sir Harry had done for them or for their children or for their grandchildren.

And what was so moving about the letters was not simply the catalogue of successful operations which had restored mobility to so many, but the affection for the man himself. It was not only his skill as a surgeon to which the letters were testimony, but his warmth as a man.

'His greatness was his goodness,' said one correspondent. 'I never met a better man,' said another.

The official obituaries of Sir Harry Platt, Bt., LL.D., M.D., M.S., F.R.C.S., for the most part, omitted that.

March/April 1987

High Risk,
Low Priority

When two frail old women are beaten and robbed in their own home, public opinion is rightly outraged. Too many old people are being attacked, and in truth one is too many.

But the debate that recent events has provoked, both in the Commons and in the media, has concentrated on the causes of such senseless attacks and the appropriate punishment. Too little attention has been given to the very vulnerability of the elderly, and to how they can be protected.

The savage attacks hit the headlines; the quiet helplessness too often goes unnoticed.

Most old people living at home and not in a home are perfectly capable of looking after themselves, but there is a growing number of the very elderly who are vulnerable because they are frail. And among the people who care there is now a serious discussion about what best can be done to help them.

It is not easy to define who are the old people at risk although I think we can all recognise them. Some may be beginning to show signs of losing their grip on reality, but most of them are vulnerable because they are dependent physically or emotionally or financially on others. And consequently at risk of abuse or maltreatment or neglect.

We all know it can happen.

Age Concern, which has initiated this whole debate, issued a very long definition which I shall paraphrase.

The people at risk, it said, are in need of support or help or advice to prevent or postpone personal deterioration or breakdown. Without help their dependence on others or their ability to manage their own lives can deteriorate to the point where they

47

might have to be put in a home. And given a choice they don't want that.

So what can be done?

Those seeking an answer have turned first to the provisions for child care – where there is much legislation – to see if anything can be learned from that, and perhaps borrowed.

Many old people will bridle at the very thought of that. Frail we may be, they will say, but we are not in our second childhood; we are adults.

Eric Midwinter, the director of the Centre for Policy on Ageing (and the man I would most like to interview on Midsummer's Day) has the answer to that.

Vulnerable elderly people, he says, are vulnerable because they are vulnerable not because they are elderly. Just as vulnerable children are vulnerable because they are at risk, not because they are young.

And the contrast between elderly people at risk and young people at risk is striking.

A mother unable to cope with a daughter whose behaviour has become a source of real anxiety can approach the local authority confident that she will get a sympathetic hearing and that something can be done. There may be occasional (and much publicised) blunders but good deeds are accomplished every day, and rightly so.

A daughter whose mother has become too much of a handful can have no such confidence that help will be forthcoming. Indeed, at a time when resources are scarce she is more likely to be imprisoned in her role. You had better give up work and look after your mother full-time, they will say.

And that is not fair.

It is not even a sensible husbanding of resources, because if the mother finally becomes too much for the daughter, the authority will then be saddled with the greater cost of institutional care.

What we need for the elderly is access to the same kind of support and advice already practised in child care. Then the social services can identify the old people at risk of abuse or self neglect or exploitation by others, and do something about it. They can also investigate the complaints, which may well be justified, of worried neighbours.

48

But the elderly are adults and however frail they may become they must never lose the right to say, No thank you – please do not interfere in my life.

Equally, if the authorities are to take on greater responsibility for the elderly but are then prevented from taking action, they cannot be blamed if a tragedy occurs which they were doing their best to prevent.

When I read about such tragedies, I often wonder whether there ought not to be an equivalent of the NSPCC for the elderly – STOPCOP perhaps, the Society to Prevent Cruelty to Old People. But in fact we have enough agencies. What they need is both more support and more powers.

It is not an easy matter to determine what to do for the best. Those who are studying it recognise that there are moral and legal and social and financial difficulties to be resolved. They know that they must examine issues of consent, representation, protection, independence, and choice.

But they also know that we cannot leave the elderly at risk.

Relatives are not always the saviours; they are sometimes the source of the unhappiness. Neighbours are not always helpful; they are sometimes the cause of friction.

Tender and loving care is not always on tap. It has to be provided, if necessary by statute.

May/June 1987

The Point
of Contact

My favourite agony aunt, who has long since retired, often upset the readers of the evening newspaper which published her regular column by ticking them off for wallowing in their loneliness.

Are you sure that it is not your own fault? she would write in reply to a reader's letter. Are you too fond of keeping yourself to yourself?

She was not being heartless, for to my knowledge she spent every hour helping people in distress, but she never lapsed into sentimentality. Many a person, she would say, is lonely because he or she makes no effort to reach out to others.

And she would certainly have agreed with a friend of mine, herself no stranger to sorrow, who argues that old ladies who sit shivering in front of daytime television waiting for Meals on Wheels would often be better off if the ingredients were delivered instead and they had to set about making their own meals. It would give them something to do.

But my favourtie agony aunt was also one of the first to realise that it was getting only too easy to lapse into loneliness. Overspill, high-rise housing, social mobility, increased divorce – these and many other changes have left more and more old people on their own. And what they lack most of all is company.

I do not for a moment believe that there was a golden age in the past when no old person was ever alone and neglected. You have only to read *The Classic Slum* or any novel by Dickens to realise that even though people lived cheek by jowl it was not all good neighbours and kind hearts.

But it does seem easier now to become isolated. Some of the loneliest people are said to be not the old and the poor but the semi-detached young housewives trapped amid the uncut moquette. And even young children now, it seems to me, spend too much time in the backs of cars, while their mothers rush from aerobics to tap-dancing class, and too little time playing with children of their own age.

But the real victims are people like Lily. Lily is eighty-seven – she was born in 1900. She lives alone in a second-floor flat. There is a lift but it takes a long time to come and Lily takes a long time to answer the door.

She is a widow with one daughter, who lives eighty miles away, and visits her mother only occasionally. Lily's only visitor is an elderly neighbour. Lily nursed her husband through a long illness and still misses him very much.

She has severe arthritis, walks slowly with a walking frame, and cannot leave her flat without help. She enjoys knitting and listening to the radio. But she is very lonely.

I have never met Lily. I came across her in a brochure published by Contact to celebrate its twenty-first birthday. Contact, which describes itself as a simple act of friendship, is a charity which exists to provide companionship for lonely and isolated people, like Lily. In its own words, it drives away loneliness.

Contact is a good idea, and it was the idea of Trevor Lyttleton, who founded it and is now its chairman.

His idea was to bring together a handful of elderly people, who were living without family support and were unable to get out without assistance, and a handful of volunteers from the same area. The volunteers would collect the old people one Sunday afternoon a month, take them to tea in someone's house, and then run them back home.

He started with one group of twelve volunteers. There are now 180 groups with 4,000 volunteers providing more than 3,000 Sunday afternoon outings for 2,500 old people. And there are new groups starting up every month.

The simplicity of the idea is that no one need feel committed to giving up more than one Sunday afternoon a month. The beauty of the idea is that it blossoms. Far from being a chore, it becomes a pleasure.

Contact now has a host of testimonials from volunteers and old people alike. The volunteers testify that the Sunday afternoon outings have enriched their lives with new friendships, and the elderly confess that the outings give them both something to enjoy and something to look forward to.

What would we do without each other? said one organiser. That would appear to sum up the achievement of Contact. It has become important in all their lives.

And the secret is the autonomy of each group. No two groups are alike, their only common denominator, as Trevor says, is shared enjoyment and informal friendship.

Many of them are not content to meet only once a month and far greater involvement between the old people and the volunteers develops spontaneously.

But they decide for themselves. Contact is a good idea, but it is something more than a good deed. It is people reaching out to each other, driving out loneliness.

Contact: 15 Henrietta Street, Covent Garden, London WC2.

July/August 1987

Doing Good,
Not Do-Gooding

'Don't,' said the doctor daughter of a friend of mine when her father announced that he was thinking of taking early retirement. 'Don't give it all up,' she said. 'It could be the death of you.' So he took her advice and is now engaged in work which is less strenuous than his previous executive responsibilities, but none the less fulfilling.

His daughter was right. An abrupt change from a busy working life to an unprepared retirement can be the death of you. I sometimes think that retirement should carry a government health warning. It can damage your health.

Daily work may be a sweat but it has many virtues, in addition to providing an income, and the first is that it gets you out of the house. How many times have you heard a woman say of her retired husband: 'I can't do with him under my feet all day'? And however helpful he may try to be, they both know that lending a hand in the house is no substitute for what he used to accomplish.

It is even more true of a career woman. They are used not only to handling a full-time job but also to coping with domestic arrangements, and for them sudden retirement can be very empty.

There are so many things that people who have been in work and who have retired miss. They miss the social companionship, the friendships and the relationships. They miss the sense of mutual obligation to fellow workers, the knowledge that they are all in it together.

They miss the recognition and the appreciation. Nothing rewards people more than a word of praise for a task accomplished and the quiet knowledge that their companions think they do a good job.

Above all they miss the sense of being useful. Work is a demonstration of purpose and of purpose achieved. A man who has had a bad day at work will say ruefully: 'I've achieved nothing today.' The fear, when he retires, is that he will say that again and again every single day.

But there is no need to. Retired people can get from voluntary work all the satisfaction that they previously got from paid work – the companionship, the mutual obligation, the recognition, the sense of usefulness. And with much greater freedom.

Retired people have skills which are in great demand among voluntary organisations. Brought up in the days when double entry book keeping was thought more important than macroeconomics, they are diligent and accurate book keepers and accountants.

Because they have been at work for their working lifetimes and are likely to have been promoted, they know how to administrate. They have run offices or stores or factories or whole businesses, and are not daunted by the size of a voluntary enterprise.

Best of all they have experience, for which there is no substitute. They know how to go about things. They know how the system works, because they have worked it.

But when they take up voluntary work they often discover that there are better ways of going about work than they ever were allowed to practise before retirement. Then they were invariably slaves to a timetable and a task, but no longer.

Voluntary work is how all work ought to be organised. The people involved choose what they want to do, how much they want to do, and when they want to do it. And in choosing what they want to do, they can either continue to practise their hard-earned skills or try their hands at something completely new while they are still able.

And so retirement becomes not a retreat but an advance.

All this, you may argue, is fine in theory but is it true in reality? Is there enough voluntary work to provide everyone who is attracted to it with the opportunity to take it up? The answer is Yes, and this will be demonstrated nationally in November.

The Volunteer Centre UK, which is the national advisory agency on volunteer and community involvement, has a confer-

As a baby in his father Leonard's arms

As a 1940 evacuee to Northumberland

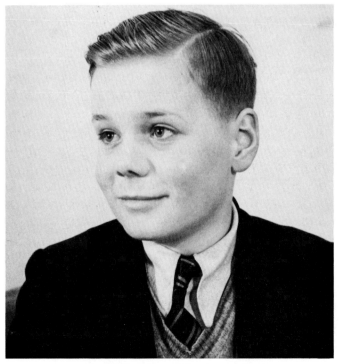

At Royal Grammar School, Newcastle

Jamming

Playing the clarinet at school

With Jenni

Wedding Bells

At the wheel of his first car *(Mercury News)*

Chairman of *Points North* *(BBC)*

With (from left) Cecil Korer, John Cohen, Estelle Roberts, Olive Shapley, Dee Wells, Joyce Howard and June Green, taking part in the BBC programme 'Something to Read' *(BBC)*

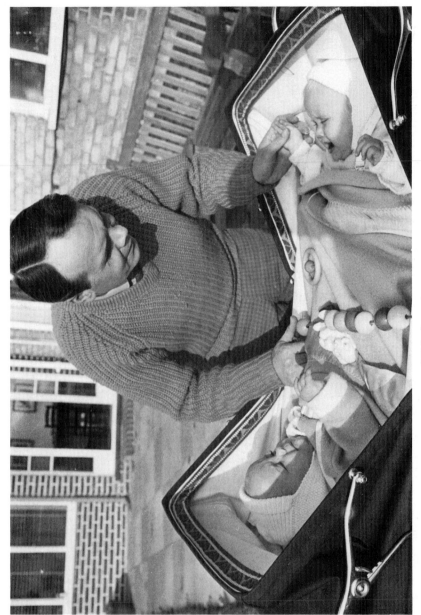

With the twins

At his farewell party from the *Guardian*

With Neville Cardus (left) and Geoffrey Mather

Taking the mickey

With Frank Mellor on location for
Home Ground

Making a *Pipeline* programme on a BP oil-rig

ence every year where traditionally it celebrates the work done by volunteers. This year it thought it would be a good idea to encourage a sequence of events in early November to coincide with its conference and the events might add up to a National Volunteer Week.

It consulted a number of national voluntary organisations and they were almost all hugely enthusiastic. So the first week of November will be National Volunteer week. The organisations which will stage events range from Dr Barnado's and the National Children's Home to the Samaritans and Age Concern.

It will be a great opportunity for the nation to recognise and to applaud the work done by volunteers and to increase public awareness of the great range of voluntary work.

But awareness is not enough. It is action that is required. And the organisers hope that National Volunteer Week will inspire many more people to take up voluntary work.

This is a recruitment campaign. The nation needs more voluntary workers for there is so much to be done. And this is doing good not do-gooding.

There are no figures to prove it, but I would wager that those who extend and taper off their working lives by voluntary work live longer and healthier lives than those who stop work abruptly on retirement.

And it gets them out of the house.

October 1987

All Change
at Crewe

I spent a large part of the only fine weekend in midsummer standing on Crewe Station. It was the first weekend in July and I was there not to catch a train but to watch the trains, and to join in the celebrations to mark the 150th birthday of Crewe.

It was on July 4, 1837, that the first train of the new Grand Junction Railway ran through Crewe, and remembered to stop. Within a few years Crewe was not only a railway station and a railway junction but a railway works and a railway town. This summer saw the opening of the Crewe Heritage Centre, and it is not to be missed.

The first passenger railway in the world was the Liverpool and Manchester Railway. It opened in 1830 and was soon followed by the London and Birmingham. Then somebody had the bright idea of joining the two and they chose the shortest route between A and B, or more precisely between B (Birmingham) and W (Warrington). Warrington was the midpoint of the L and M, halfway between Liverpool and Manchester, and when the new line reached it that was a Grand T-Junction. A station was built on the new line at the point where the Manchester to Nantwich Road crossed (it still does) and they called the station Crewe after the stately home, Crewe Hall.

Within five years Crewe Station became Crewe Junction. New lines converged on it from all sides – from Chester, from Manchester, from Staffordshire, from Shropshire – and then those lines too extended to Carlisle and Scotland, and to Wales and Holyhead, it was true to say that from Crewe you could get a train to every corner of the kingdom. And it was likely to be a Crewe train, pulled by a locomotive built in the railway works located in the crock of the Warrington and Chester lines, right beside the station, and now the site of the new Heritage Centre.

It was the railway works not the railway junction that created the need for a railway station. The workers in the Works had to live somewhere and the station was surrounded by green fields. So the railway company hired an architect, a Mr John Cunningham, and he laid out a new town for the workers of the company to live in.

They came with their families from the slums of Liverpool and from the poor villages of North Wales, and they could not believe their good fortune. Instead of the squalor and poverty they had left behind, they found rows of neat four-roomed cottages, with little gardens at the back, with sewers and running water, with gas laid on by the company gasworks – all for two shillings a week rent plus twopence a week for the gas. And that was only for the labourers. There were double fronted houses for the foremen, and villas for the works superintendents.

Those new houses were not only far removed from the slums, there was also no fear of their becoming slums. It was a condition not only of tenancy that the tenants keep their company houses clean and tidy, it was also a condition of employment. Anyone who allowed his home to become filthy and disreputable was dismissed. Which is one reason why so many of those first houses are still a joy to behold.

The railway company also built a church for its workers. It too still stands – or rather half of it does. From a distance it looks like a fine stone building. Close to, you discover that the fabric is brickwork cunningly faced with stone where it shows, and the pillars are cast iron painted to resemble stone. But it's the thought that counts.

Not everyone, of course, was C of E, so the company also helped other denominational groups to build chapels and there were seventeen in all ranging from the Calvinistic Methodists to the Particular Baptists. There was also a brothel in Cross Street. The company tried to run everything in Crewe. It built a Mechanics Institute and sought to ban radical newspapers from the reading room, but the workers objected. In the early 1880s the company tried to use its power to force the men to vote Conservative in the local election. It became known as the period of The Intimidation, but the men were not to be intimidated and the company in future decided to keep out of politics.

But it could never keep out of Crewe because it was Crewe, and in the year 1887, when the company's fiftieth anniversary coincided with Queen Victoria's Jubilee, the company – in the person of Francis Webb, Chief Engineer of the Works, Mayor of the Town, and commonly referred to as the King of Crewe – gave the town a park, Queen's Park. And it too is still a fine monument to Crewe's achievement.

Indeed it was that gesture and that celebration a hundred years ago which inspired the present municipal council to make the most of the 150th anniversary. And this time they too decided that they would not only have an event but something more lasting. The event was a huge success. On that glorious warm weekend people came in their hundreds to tour both the Works, which is still in production, and the new Heritage Centre. They marvelled, as I did, at the old locomotives and at the enthusiasm of those who maintain them.

But the Crewe Heritage Centre is more than an exercise in nostalgia, more than an excuse to tell the young about the old days. It is an exercise in self-esteem, an opportunity for people to discover for themselves what a fascinating place Crewe was, and is, so that they may be inspired to make even more of it.

John Bedson, the councillor who chairs the Heritage Sub-Committee, is himself a refined railwayman of railway stock. His father, his grandfather and his great-grandfather worked in the railways at Crewe before him. His great-great-grandfather was one of the first to walk from the coast of North Wales to Crewe to find work (and a home) there. John Bedson knows that Crewe has had a remarkable past, but he is equally determined that it will have a remarkable future. The new Heritage Centre is the signal of that determination.

November 1987

My Old Mate Should Stay Up North

The oldest man I know – or to be more accurate the earliest man I know – was born three hundred years before Christ. He is a neighbour of mine and his many friends round here are worried about where he will spend this Christmas. His name is Lindow Man, though there are those who, rather impertinently, call him Pete Marsh. He lived in the Iron Age and his body was found three years ago in a peat bog called Lindow Moss near Wilmslow here in Cheshire not far from Rainow where I live.

Lindow Man was a Celt and almost certainly a priest or a sacrificial victim. His body when found was remarkably preserved but had evidence of a blow on the head and a cord round his neck. He was only twenty-five when he died.

The Celts were a funny lot, not easy to understand. 'To believe that we can penetrate the Celtic mind is a pure waste of time,' wrote one distinguished historian in despair. They were a savage, vain, high-spirited people, given to riding across Europe with the skulls of their defeated enemies attached to their belts. They occupied lands from the Black Sea to the Atlantic – when Lindow Man was alive – but they were not empire builders.

They were united only in language, religion, and culture, and their more organised enemies, like the Romans, were able eventually to defeat them. The Romans never conquered Ireland which was why Celtic civilisation took root there eventually to produce Celtic Christian saints. But that was long after Lindow Man's time. He was a well brought up young man with the delicate hands of one not bred for toil. Perhaps he was always intended for sacrifice to propitiate one god or another.

For month after month this year people have come in their thousands to Manchester Museum to see him and to learn about him. They have shuddered at the account of his ritual execution, and marvelled at the description of life in Cheshire 2300 years ago. Then they were told that Lindow Man was to be moved to London. Over our dead bodies, they said, and a great campaign erupted. He is one of us, he is ours, he belongs here, they said. The North/South divide was never more divided. They are stealing our dead now, said one Northern woman bitterly.

The 'they' to whom she was referring are the people at the British Museum in London. They argue that the discovery of Lindow Man is of such international importance for scholarship and education that he should be shown alongside other similar material and shown to the widest possible audience. Where better than the British Museum, they say, and a special room for Lindow Man is being prepared.

What nonsense, says the chorus from the North. Manchester Museum has already won an award for its skill in displaying Lindow Man. Two thousand people a day have come to see him. Furthermore they have then been able to go on to visit Lindow Moss, where he was found, and Tatton Park, where there are the remains of the Celtic village in which he may even have lived.

It is, argue people in Manchester and the North West, typical of London to assume that everything of national importance must be housed there. They already have more than enough. There is truth in that argument made all the more compelling by the success of specialist museums and exhibitions throughout the country.

I could name dozens: Beamish, Bowes, the National Railway Museum at York, the National Museum of Photography at Bradford, Castleford in Manchester, and the National Museums and Galleries in Merseyside. When Kenneth Hudson, who is probably the world's greatest authority on museums, was asked in a recent interview which was his favourite, he replied: Quarry Bank Mill Museum at Styal in Cheshire.

Quarry Bank Mill is only a mile or two from where Lindow Man was found. It is one of a network of museums in the North West which guarantee their visitors a fascinating day. A Lindow Man Museum centred upon the Man himself and devoted to his time and his people should be where he lived.

Like Tollund Man, he is said to have the best preserved head of an early man to have been found anywhere in the world, and

Tollund Man is in a museum in Central Jutland down the road from where he was found. There was no question of his going to the National Museum in Copenhagen.

Lindow Man should not go to London either, on anything other than a return ticket.

December 1987

Tourism is Good
for All

I am a resident.
You are a holiday maker.
He is a tourist.

You will recognise the snobbery. Tourism is, or was, a dirty word. Saga, which knows a thing or two about tourism, is none the less careful to call itself Saga Holidays. Holidays are an escape; tourism, too often, is seen as an invasion. But tourism is a two-way trade in which, I believe, both sides benefit.

The new Minister of Tourism wrote to me a month or two ago to say that in going through the bits and pieces left behind by his predecessor, he had come across a document written by me long before Mrs Thatcher came to power and called 'Tourism is . . .' It was written to encourage the tourist trade in the North West of England and was intended as a statement of the essentials. It began with a list of the benefits of tourism:

Tourism is good for you,
- it brings in money and trade,
- it creates jobs and checks depopulation,
- it inspires the preservation and improvement of the good things of the past,
- it prompts the development of better services, facilities and amenities for visitor and inhabitant alike,
- it enriches the environment,
- it restores pride in place,
AND – it makes people happy.

That I still believe is the essence of it. Properly managed, tourism is good for the economy, good for the environment, and good for people. But badly managed, without planning and control, tourism can create overcrowding and congestion, pollution and noise, erosion and squalor, and vandalism and litter.

Fifteen years ago the tourist industry in Britain had many problems. It was short of cash, short of staff, short of sympathy. Its year was too short and its day was too long. It lacked friends in high places. It had yet to persuade the authorities, both local and national, that it is big business, crucial to the welfare and prosperity of the community.

It has come a long way since then. No one sneers at tourism now though they are occasionally rude about tourists, especially in London. And yet there is no greater compliment than someone coming from abroad to visit and enjoy your country.

When the Greater London Council was abolished and it became known that local government had no further use for County Hall, which is across the Thames from the Palace of Westminster, I wrote to Mrs Thatcher suggesting that it should become the National Tourist Centre.

She wrote back and said that she could not, or would not, spend taxpayer's money on such a venture, and drew my attention to the new tourist office in Lower Regent Street. It is very attractive but it is a corner shop compared with what I had in mind.

I envisaged County Hall as the place where every visitor to London would go on his or her first day in the capital. It would house the headquarters of all the national tourist bodies, the British Tourist Authority and the English Tourist Board, the London offices of the Scottish, Wales and Northern Ireland Tourist Boards. It would house the London Tourist Board itself and be a shopwindow for all the regional tourist boards. It would not be an office block but a great information centre, rich with exhibitions and video displays, showing the visitor all the good things that Britain has to offer. It would be a great exercise in national self-esteem. (Saga would be there too).

But I fear it is not to happen, and County Hall will become yet one more hotel, and a great opportunity will have been lost. It is not so everywhere. All around Britain, not least in the North West of England where I live, more and more places which a few years ago were dismissed as dumps, have been restored to the delight of locals and visitors alike.

The Castleford area of Manchester, which I have mentioned here before, used to look like the place where the bomb had dropped, and is now an urban heritage park attracting people by the thousand. Wigan Pier which was once a joke is now a joy. Albert Dock at Liverpool will soon house the Tate Gallery of the North to add to the five great museums and galleries of Merseyside.

All that is tourism. Successful tourism involves the identification of the most appropriate tourist activity for the locality. The successful promotion of tourism involves making something happen, making it known, and making it easy to visit.

There is no better example of this than the town of Lowell in Massachusetts. John Cabot Lowell came to Oldham in 1811 and went back home to build a mill town like it. Lowell was the first prosperous industrial town in New England. But twenty years ago it was run down and people could not wait to get away from it. Now its fortunes have been restored. Downtown Lowell is the first urban National Park in America. The canal system is in use again, the trolley cars run again, the mill buildings are occupied again. And last year a million visitors came to see it.

Tourism can be overdone. Careless developments without thought for the consequences can overwhelm a place and destroy its attractiveness. But thoughtful tourism and thoughtful tourists add up to fulfilment.

I tried to say it all, all those years ago, in one couplet:

Tourism can spoil or can enhance,
But it cannot be left to chance.

January/February 1988

Beginning to
Bother

'Left to itself, to the wind and the rain, to the birds and the bees, to the wildlife in the woods, but untouched by human hand, Britain would be something of a wilderness.

'The high peaks would rise above it all, the sunset over the Western Isles would be undiminished, but there would be no one to enjoy it.

'We the people, creators and spectators, make all the difference.

'But we do sometimes overdo it . . .'

Those are the opening words of a film which I wrote as a contribution to EYE, the European Year of the Environment, which is just drawing to a close. If you ever get to see the film, you will hear those words spoken by Hannah Gordon.

I wrote the film essentially to make the point that Earth and Man were made for each other. Alone among the species on this planet, human beings both acknowledge the wonders of Nature and seek to improve on them. To the other living creatures the Earth is simply a habitat and they make the best of it as it is. To us it is an environment which we seek, for better or for worse, to change. And nowhere is this more evident than in Britain.

Much of Britain is a monument to good works, to the patient labour of men and women over the centuries, cultivating the land, tidying up the homestead, proclaiming their ingenuity and their faith. Every unspoiled village is a human creation, not a natural phenomenon. All the things we show off to visitors – the ancient earth works and the stone circles, the medieval castles and the cathedral closes, the eighteenth century waterways and the nineteenth century seaside piers – are man-made.

You could spend every holiday in a lifetime touring Britain

and still not see everything that is worth seeing. There is so much to admire and to enjoy. But if you look the other way, it is a very different picture.

It began to go wrong two centuries ago. Some people had always made a mess, but usually in their own back yards. The Industrial Revolution changed all that. The move from attic and workshop to mill and factory was not only the greatest change in human life in recorded history, it also made the greatest mess.

Not at first. People flocked to see the new mills, for they were as handsome as stately homes. But soon the smoke from countless chimneys clogged the air of industrial Britain. And the filth from countless factories fouled the rivers. Houses were slums, rivers sewers, the air smog.

In places where there was little or no industry, there was no industrial pollution, but there was little or no work either. People either starved or emigrated. But where there was industry there was work and there was also the means to overcome the very difficulties industry was creating. People began to apply the same ingenuity and enterprise to water supply and sanitation, to smoke control and anti-pollution, to slum clearance and to public health, that they had to manufacturing, and the wealth from manufacturing industry helped to finance the new services. Not that it always happened. Sometimes people were ignorant of the damage they were doing. Sometimes not enough people appeared to care. Sometimes they left the mess behind and moved on.

Cities overspilled, their populations often rehoused in places where they didn't want to be, in houses they didn't want to live in. And overspill did nothing for the inner cities or for the people left behind in them. The rundown and relocation of the industry left nothing for those still living where the industry used to be. If a place is a dump, the people in it grow despairing. Why bother? they say, or worse.

But at last we are bothering. We are beginning to clear up the mess, some of it the errors of two centuries, some of it the result of recent neglect. Everywhere people want the place to look better and to feel better and to be better. And as we move into a new Industrial Age there is seen to be less and less excuse for industrial squalor and pollution and dereliction. The new methods of manufacture need not leave a mess. And the new factories which house them glisten and gleam in parkland settings. They can make money without muck.

But there are new horrors – new chemicals which, if allowed to escape, can poison the air or kill the rivers, new pesticides which can kill everything except the crop, of which there is sometimes too much. There are new roads adding to the thunder of traffic, and old roads choked with vehicles pumping out exhaust fumes into designated smokeless zones. And always the fear of the silent unseen leak of radiation, where a single accident can harm the world.

We cannot say that we have not been warned. This time round we need to know what we are doing. This is not a post-industrial Britain that we now live in, but it is a new Industrial Britain. We still need industry if we are to prosper and pay for the improvements to our surroundings. What matters now is that we should be an industrial nation with nothing to hide.

March 1988

Roots of the American Dream

'I never knew that,' said a lady in a letter from San Francisco, 'and I have lived here all my life.' Her confession was prompted by a television programme she had just seen. In it I had argued that Northern Ireland is the home of the American dream.

It is the ancestral home of the people who are known in America as the Scotch-Irish. They are the descendants of the Presbyterians from Scotland who settled in Ulster in the seventeenth century at the behest of King James the First. These Ulster Scots became Ulstermen. But in the eighteenth century 250,000 of them left Ulster. They left because the English thwarted everything they held dear – their agriculture, their industry, and their religion. They were denied markets and office and religious freedom, so they upped and they left. They sailed across the Atlantic to America. And they became Americans.

They were the instrument and the inspiration of its independence, its expansion and its dreams. They were the frontiersmen – Daniel Boone and Davy Crockett were among them. And if you visit the Ulster American Folk Park at Camphill in County Tyrone you will see how and why.

Theodore Roosevelt, whose mother, Martha Bulloch, came from County Antrim, said of them: 'They were a grim stern people, strong and simple, knowing neither ruth nor pity. They were of all men best fitted to conquer the wilderness and hold it against all comers.'

The Old World they left and the New World they built had much in common, because they took with them their way of life, their love of religion and of learning, and their covered wagons. They settled in Pennsylvania, in West Virginia, in the Carolinas.

Some went south to Georgia and others pushed inland to Kentucky and Tennessee.

By 1776 there were no fewer than 123 Ulster Presbyterian settlements in America, and Benjamin Franklin said they were in a fair way to taking possession of the State. And when it came to the crunch, the Ulstermen were not torn like the English settlers between love of the old country and the colonial cause, they were the servants and the soldiers of the American Revolution.

George Washington said that if defeated he would make his last stand for liberty among the Scotch-Irish. His Secretary of War was James McHenry from Ballymena; his greatest soldier was General Henry Knox whose father came from Londonderry.

Five Ulstermen put their names to the Declaration of Independence and a sixth printed it. He was John Dunlap, who had learned his trade at a printing shop in Strabane which is still there to this day. He wrote home and said that the young men of Ireland should come to America because there was no place in the world 'where a man meets so rich a reward for conduct and industry'.

Thomas Mellon left a log cabin in Ulster at the age of five for another log cabin in Turtle Creek, Pennsylvania. He became a judge and a banker and the father of Andrew Mellon, secretary to the US Treasury, and in his time the richest man in America. Mellon money restored the old homestead in Ulster and you can find it in the middle of a folk park.

But the contribution of Ulster Protestants to American history is best displayed in the catalogue of Presidents. Men of direct Ulster descent occupied the White House for fifty-six of the ninety-two years between the inauguration of Andrew Jackson and the termination of Woodrow Wilson's eight years in office. Andrew Jackson's parents lived in the village of Boneybefore and his mother was with child when they sailed from Carrickfergus.

The family of James Knox Polk came from Londonderry. The family of James Buchanan from Deroran in County Tyrone. The family of Andrew Johnson from Larne in County Antrim. Hannah Simpson, the mother of Ulysees S. Grant, was born in Auchmocloy in County Tyrone. William Arthur, the father of Chester Alan Arthur, was born at Cullybacky in County Antrim.

Grover Cleveland's mother was the daughter of Abner Neal

who emigrated from County Antrim. Cleveland had two terms as President with a break of four years between. Benjamin Harrison was President in those four years and his family too came from Ulster. Cleveland was then succeeded by William McKinley, the great-great-grandson of James McKinley who left a farm in Conagher, County Antrim, to sail to America in 1743. The farm is still called McKinley's Farm.

Woodrow Wilson's grandfather served his apprenticeship in the very same printing shop in Strabane which employed John Dunlap. I like to think that it was Dunlap's letter which persuaded James Wilson to emigrate. On board ship he met a girl called Annie Adams from a nearby village. They married and had ten children. The tenth they called Joseph, and it was his son Woodrow who became the tenth President of the United States whose family came from Ulster.

Today there are 20,000,000 people in the United States whose surnames are Wilson or Jackson or Thompson or Simpson or Taylor or Logan or Blair and whose roots are in Northern Ireland.

'I never knew that,' said the lady in San Francisco, but she does now.

April 1988

70

Companions
for Life

'I no longer read anything new,' said an old friend of mine recently, 'I only read old books again.'

'You always did,' I replied, for he is a man who has been set in his ways for as long as I have known him, and all the more steadfast a companion because of it. Not that his mind is closed. His judgement of contemporary political antics is both sharp and often quoted, but none the less he has little time for what is new. He defends this indifference on the grounds that what is new is probably spurious, probably obscure, and almost certainly a waste of his time.

I think he is wrong, as I keep telling him.

It is true that much that is new adds up to not very much, but it was always thus. For every forgotten masterpiece there are countless forgotten paltry pieces. The mistake is to cut short the pursuit of the good. Discovery is the great exercise of youth but it should not stop there. No one is born with a love of Mozart or of Keats or Turner. It has to be acquired and the acquisition is a great adventure.

It is what education is supposed to be about. And although it cannot and should not be left to schools alone, a good school is a good start. At ours we were doubly blessed. The music master thought that all of us could, if we bothered, not only enjoy music but play it. He was a composer and an eccentric too. He once appeared on a concert platform with the Hallé Orchestra, who had performed a piece of his, and he took his bow in his raincoat. He persuaded many of us to take up instruments, learn to play them tolerably well, and in the process come to enjoy the whole world of music, old and new. Years later, when I appeared on

Face the Music, the only pieces I recognised instantly were those we had played at school.

The chemistry master was even more remarkable. Although he taught a science his real love was poetry and he edited the famous *Faber Book of Modern Verse* which was first published in 1934. In it he introduced a large part of the nation to the verse of Eliot and Pound and Auden and Spender with these words:

'More often than prose or mathematics, poetry is received in a hostile spirit, as if its publication were an affront to the reader; yet most of the poetry which is published probably appears because, at the time of writing, it delighted the writer and convinced him that it held some profound significance or some exact description which he hoped that others, too, might see.'

He persuaded me. I started with Gerard Manley Hopkins and W.B. Yeats. (Only recently did I learn that those two, the greatest poets of their time, were only in the same room once, at an embassy party in Dublin, and no one thought fit to introduce them.)

But my favourite then was e.e. cummings, who had his own rules about capital letters and punctuation, as in this poem:

> *here's a little mouse) and*
> *what does he think about, i*
> *wonder as over this*
> *floor (quietly with*
> *bright eyes) drifts (nobody*
> *can tell because Nobody*
> *knows, . . .*

For weeks I signed all my homework b.l. redhead, until the headmaster had a word with me. But I have been reading poetry ever since, old and new. It is not a journey of nostalgia but a continuing adventure, and certainly not a pastime to be discarded.

People offer many excuses to explain why they abandon the things that once gave them real pleasure: the need to earn a living, to concentrate upon a career, to raise a family. But to cry 'No Time!' is to imitate the Mad Hatter who cried 'No Room!' A love of poetry should not begin with a first nursery rhyme and end with A-levels. Good poets are companions for life. And not

72

all good poets are dead poets. Like Chaucer's pilgrims their numbers are added to every day.

I shall never persuade my old friend of this. He thinks that poetry ended with *The Highwayman*, which he like me learned to recite at school. But there is so much more to discover. When two of our best poets, Seamus Heaney and Ted Hughes, put together an anthology recently, they mixed the old and the new and the new was not outshone. Poems are best read out loud whether to others or alone, and perhaps in bed at night where they should take second place only to prayers.

May 1988

A Mouthful
of Marmalade

There were seventeen dishes of marmalade, numbered one to seventeen, and there were three of us – a cook, a historian, and me. 'Taste those,' said the woman in charge, handing us a questionaire on which to record our preferences. Sweet or sharp, soft or stiff, syrupy or solid. I had already had a full British Rail English Breakfast, but I set to work with enthusiasm inspired by the belief that marmalade is the greatest invention since the wheel.

I suspect that women invented both; the wheel in Mesopotamia to save themselves from being beasts of burden, and marmalade in Arabia to pass a thousand and one nights. We should all be grateful for both. I like my marmalade on toast and spread an inch thick. This may seem greedy but my defence is that I was denied it during the war when there was rationing and coupons and you were only allowed a thin scraping, so I am making up for all those years. I like it open to the heavens and not suppressed in a sandwich, though I can see that Paddington Bear needs marmalade sandwiches if he insists on keeping them in his hat.

I had to appear more fastidious at the great tasting so I simply popped a dollop of each marmalade on seventeen small pieces of brown bread and butter and set to work. It was a labour of love. I swallowed each in turn, totted up the points I had awarded, and pronounced number fifteen the winner. To my delight, my companions, who had taken a little longer, agreed. And who would dare dispute the unaminous verdict of a regular consumer, a practising cook, and a learned historian?

As a reward for my efforts I came away with a pot of marmalade and *The Book of Marmalade*, the latter, the work of the aforesaid historian. From it I discovered that marmalade – both the word and the deed – came to Britain from Portugal. The first recorded cargo of it arrived at the Port of London on March 10, 1495, in a ship belonging to Farnando Yanes. I have it in mind to nominate March 10, 1995, as National Marmalade Day to celebrate 500 years of marmalade eating.

The Portugese had learned how to make it from the Moors, for its origins are Arabic, though the Greeks and the Romans knew of it too, and the Persians had a sweet tooth. All of them made their marmalade from quinces, not from oranges, and it was this quince conserve which came to England nicely in time to adorn Tudor dinner tables. It was a noble's dish then, as well as a noble dish, served towards the end of a meal, stiff and sliced.

It was thought to be very good for you. 'Taken after meat,' wrote one scholar, 'it closeth and draweth the stomach together . . . and mollifyeth the belly, if it be abundantly taken.' Mary, Queen of Scots, took it abundantly, to combat sea-sickness.

It was also thought to be an aphrodisiac. 'Thou art as witty a marmalade-eater as ever I conversed with,' said a Lord to his loved one and it was taken as a compliment. And another excused a kiss refused with these words: 'I cannot blame my lady's unwillingness to part with such marmalade lips.' I trust the pair of them came to a sticky end.

But when marmalade went down market and was eaten by the poor, 'marmalade madams' was slang for women of easy virtue. By then the orange had replaced the quince, and there were two types of marmalade, one made from beaten oranges, the other with the peel added in shreds or chips. But it was still a dessert, served in a glass, alongside syllabub and jelly and fruit cream.

It was the Scots who first served it for breakfast. They were looking for something to warm the stomach. They still began the day with a dram of whisky but instead of following that with mulled ale they took marmalade instead and drank tea. They had more marmalade on oatcakes when they drank tea in the evening.

So when a Spanish ship loaded with oranges took shelter in Dundee harbour one day towards the end of the eighteenth century, Janet Keiller, the daughter of a grocer, saw her chance. She set up business with her son James as marmalade makers and established chip marmalade, as distinct from beaten or smooth marmalade, as Scotland's own. That was in 1797. So we can have another National Marmalade Day in 1997.

Once the Keillers got going everyone was at it, north and south of the border. The wife of another grocer, Marion Robertson of Paisley, whose husband James had acquired a barrel of Seville oranges which he could not sell, turned them into 'Golden Shred.' The Baxters, George the grocer and his wife Margaret, who had been in service in Gordon Castle, set themselves up in a grocery business at Fochabers in Morayshire, and Margaret made marmalade, and famous jams too.

In England, Frank Cooper, yet another grocer, started selling his Oxford marmalade, made by his wife, Sarah Jane, in 1874. Chivers, of Histon, a farming family in Cambridgeshire, borrowed cooks from Pembroke College, Cambridge, to get into the business. The fruit farmers, seeing where the profit was, took up marmalade making themselves. Arthur Wilkin of Tiptree was one, Sir Water Gilbey of Elsenham Hall, another. And of course, more and more people made their own. And still do, to judge from the number of pots I have received in the post since the results of the great tasting were made public.

Even the Europeans, who foolishly prefer bread and jam for breakfast, are learning better. And the Japanese, or so I am assured, are taking to it. There has been some back sliding in Britain, people putting their muesli where their mouths are. It can only end in national anorexia. So spread the word, and spread the marmalade – an inch thick.

June 1988

Rambling in
the Kinder Way

O n the first fine Sunday this summer, a large number of
elderly people gathered in a quarry in Derbyshire and sang
a battle song. Its chorus startled the rooks and enchanted the
onlookers.

> *I'm a rambler, I'm a rambler*
> *from Manchester way;*
> *I get all my pleasure the hard*
> *moorland way;*
> *I may be a wage slave on*
> *Monday*
> *But I am a free man on*
> *Sunday.*

The singers, most of whom have long ceased to be wage slaves,
and many of whom can only ramble a step or two now, had
gathered to celebrate the Kinder Trespass, the mass act of
defiance which began in that same quarry on that same Sunday
in April, fifty-six years ago. Twenty of the original trespassers
were there with their friends and their relatives and with
countless more of their contemporaries who had come to salute
their achievement. And to enjoy the sunshine.

Beneath a permanent plaque which records that the Mass
Trespass of Kinder Scout started from Bowden Bridge Quarry a
mile out of Hayfield, the leader of that Trespass, Benny Roth-
man, addressed the crowd, and they hung on to his every word.
Benny, who is a year or two short of eighty, and an inch or two
short of five feet, is still a rambler on foot, but straight to the
point in speech. He told the story of that day – the trespass on to

the forbidden moorland, the fights with the gamekeepers, the arrests by the police. Benny was one of the five who subsequently went to prison.

Almost everyone in his audience already knew the story of that famous day (all ramblers do) but to hear it from Benny himself, standing there in breeches and yellow stockings, like something out of Shakespeare, was not only to recall it again but to re-live it. Not that everyone among those assembled approved. Some think the Trespass was a great irrelevance. They said so at the time and they argue with Benny to this day. It deflected attention, they say, from the serious business of negotiating access to the moorland countryside.

But others, and I am one of them, think it must have concentrated minds wonderfully. It laid claim to a right, a right then denied but soon after to be conceded, at least in principle. It certainly had an effect on sensitive people at the time, as visitors to the recent festival in Manchester of the music of Sir Michael Tippett were reminded.

The festival brochure told the story of Tippett's first visit to Manchester, which, as it happened, was in April 1932. Tippett came to see his friend from student days, David Ayerst, who was then a reporter on the Manchester Guardian, and many years later was to write the history of that great newspaper. Ayerst was sent to report the Trespass so Tippett went with him, and to this day can recall the rows of keepers silhouetted against the sky at the top of Kinder Scout. When the ramblers swarmed the slopes Tippett went with them and was hit with a stone thrown by a gamekeeper. Ayerst's press pass saved the pair of them from arrest, but the incident had a profound effect on Tippett. It showed him something of the divisions in society then, of the haves and the have-nots, and a few days later he decided to join an organisation which was seeking to help unemployed miners.

All this was discussed after the outdoor rally in the Quarry at an indoor rally in the pub, the Royal Hotel in Hayfield. Speaker after speaker applauded the original trespassers (who were modest and witty about their exploits) and then went on to categorise the threats to the countryside today, and the obstacles to access – indiscriminate planting of conifers, privatisation of water, inappropriate tourist developments. The young present repeated the old battle-cry: the right of access on foot to all open country, to protect rights of way and to protect the natural beauty of the countryside. The old agreed and showed themselves not content to settle for previous battles won.

But there were great moments of recollection and of history. Tales of how the Manchester Association for the Preservation of Ancient Footpaths, founded in 1826, became in 1894 The Peak District and Northern Counties Footpath Preservation Society. The cast-iron signposts it erected are now protected as items of historical interest. The Society still exists. It is now called the Peak and Northern Footpath Society, and when it celebrates its centenary in 1994 Benny intends to be there – probably in the same pub.

There was talk too of the great Tom Stephenson, the prince of ramblers, who disapproved of the Mass Trespass, but who none the less chose the same day in April when the time came to open his Pennine Way, the finest footpath in the land. Tom battled with authority for thirty years to fulfill his dream and the Pennine Way finally opened in its entirety on April 24, 1965. In 1935 when he had first proposed a Pennine Way, Tom had said that it was 'a faint line on the Ordnance Maps which the feet of grateful pilgrims would, with the passing years, engrave on the face of the land'.

They have. Much of the Way is now worn with the steps of thousands and thousands of feet. And we talked about that too on that recent Sunday. Forgive us our Trespass, said one old gentleman, with mock contrition. But he fooled no one.

July/August 1988

What Should We Do with the Year 2000?

What, people frequently ask me, was your most embarrassing moment? They mean: on the radio. I could never think of a convincing answer because I am not easily embarrassed. But I can now.

On the day between the Queen's Birthday and St George's Day this year, I solemnly informed the nation that there were 5001 days between that day and the end of the century. I was wrong. Very wrong. By a margin of 529 days or thereabouts. It was deeply embarrassing.

It came about like this. We were gossiping in the *Today* studio one morning after the programme when a visitor asked me if I knew that there were 5001 days between St George's Day, 1988, and the end of the twentieth century. Not given to taking anything without checking, I asked him: (a) Did he mean to the end of the year 2000, not to the end of 1999, for a century, as every cricketer will tell you, requires 100 not 99, and (b) Had he included the extra days in the leap years?

Yes, he said, to both questions. His calculation extended to December 31, 2000, and he had remembered that there will be a February 29 in 1992, 1996, and 2000. Ah, said another voice in the studio, you are wrong about 2000. The century years are never leap years. From which we all deduced that there would be 5001 days between April 22, the day after the Queen's Birthday and the day before St George's Day, and the end of the century. But when I passed that information, or as they say nowadays, misinformation, on to the nation, the phones rang at once.

Idiot, said the first caller, you are more than a year out. We passed the 5001st day in 1986. More courteous callers went into greater detail, pointing out among other things that 2000 is a leap year, though 1900 was not. I had to look that up in Brewer's indispensable *Dictionary of Phrase and Fable*, and sure enough a leap year is any year whose date is divisible by four except those which are divisible by 100 but not by 400.

The explanation is fascinating. The astronomical year, the time that it takes the earth to go round the sun, is approximately 365¼ days, so an extra day every four years is only an approximate correction. The earth actually takes 365.2422 days to go round the sun, so the difference between .24(¼) and .2422 is righted by the loss of three days in four hundred years not four. If you are still baffled, consult any bright grandchild.

My howler, however, set me thinking about the end of the century. It may not be until December 31, 2000 but you can be sure that it will be celebrated in 1999. That will be the last year of the 1900s, not of the twentieth century, but we shall be bombarded with books, articles, programmes, and exhibitions – all seeking to sum up the achievement and the horrors of the century. I plan to have a go at it myself in 1999.

But if the twenty-first century does not begin until New Year's Day, 2001 what should we do with the year 2000? Should we designate it the International Year of the Environment? The year in which we face up honestly to the damage that we are doing to the planet and undertake to mend our ways? We could produce an Atlas of World Destruction showing precisely where and to what extent greed, ignorance and thoughtlessness are not only polluting the planet but robbing it of its resources. Should we go further and declare 2000 the Year of International Non-violence, a year in which nobody deliberately kills anybody else anywhere in the world? Or would the pent-up violence simply explode at some later date?

I was attempting the other day to calculate how many wars are happening in the world at present, war being defined as any declared armed conflict between organised groups of people. After my miscalculation of the century, I am reluctant to go public, but the figure is not far short of fifty. So a year of universal amnesty would be welcome.

But I know and you know that the opportunity will be missed. 2000 will be like any other year and probably worse. Round figures tend to make people reckless. It will be as much as we can do to persuade those in authority to try not to do too much damage. In the meantime you might like to calculate the date on which there will be 4001 days to the end of the century. I make it January 17, 1990, but I could be embarrassingly wrong.

September 1988

The Writing
on the Wall

L et me begin with a quiz. What have the following got in
common: gone to the wall, back to the wall, against the
wall?

Answer: they all sound threatening with their echoes of penury
and poverty and pressure.

But think of them as a holiday quiz and they sound quite
different. I was struck by that thought this summer when I
found myself inspecting perhaps the finest city wall in Europe –
one that has come full circle. In a sense I had come full circle
too, because all my life I have been fascinated by walls. I can
remember as a very small boy being taken by my grandfather to
see the Sallyport gate in the city wall which once encircled
Newcastle-upon-Tyne.

Medieval Newcastle was the most densely populated city in
England outside London, its population crammed into a city
surrounded by a wall two miles long with seven main gates,
nineteen towers, and countless turrets. But when I was a
schoolboy in Newcastle our great delight was Hadrian's Wall.

We would cycle out at the weekend, lodge in a youth hostel
and walk the Wall from Chester to Housesteads. It was like
another world, and still is.

When I first moved into the North West of England I was
much taken by the city walls of Chester. Walk those at dusk on
an autumn evening and you would swear you can hear Roman
soldiers whispering. When I went to China I made straight for
the Great Wall, along with several thousand Chinese tourists,
many of whom assured me that this was for them the great
moment of their lives. You are not grown up in China, one
explained, until you have been to the Great Wall.

The Berlin Wall is different. People turn their backs to it, on both sides. But it too goes in a circle all the way round West Berlin, one hundred miles in all. The inner city stretch separates West Berlin from the original city centre. It is as if there was a wall down Edgware Road, past Marble Arch, round the back of Buckingham Palace, and down to the Thames. If there were, all the best bits – Buckingham Palace, the Palace of Westminster, the Temple, the Tower – would be in the East.

One day, I suppose, the Berlin Wall will come down with no one clamouring for its conservation. Not so the city wall, or more precisely, the city walls I saw for the first time this summer – the walls of Lucca. I have been to Tuscany on many occasions, to Pisa, to Siena, to Florence – all of them incomparable cities, but until this year Lucca had been for me a dot on the map or a sign on the autostrada. When for the first time I followed the sign to Lucca from the autostrada I found myself at the Elisa Gate, built by, and named after, Napoleon's sister to speed her entry into the city.

Inside Lucca, the most famous object is the Volto Santo or Holy Cross which is housed in a small temple inside the Cathedral. This crucifix, the legend says, was carved by Nicodemus himself from a cedar in Lebanon. The carving of Christ on the Cross was hidden in the Holy Land for several centuries and then put on a boat without a crew and entrusted to the sea. It sailed, guided only by the wind, to Italy where it was put on a cart drawn by wild oxen who, unattended, brought it to Lucca. In fact it was probably carved by a man in Lucca towards the end of the ninth century. But it is the symbol of the city, and centuries of smoke from candles and incense have given the whole figure a dark gloss. Every year in September the citizens of Lucca dress it in gold and carry it through the city streets in a grand-scale procession.

Almost as beautiful, I think, is a twelfth century crucifix painted on wood which hangs above the altar in the Church of San Michele. That church has a white limestone façade, which rises up and up and up in layer after layer of arcades, and it dominates the piazza which was once the Roman forum. All these – the crosses, the churches, the narrow streets, the piazzas, especially the elliptical piazza that was once the Roman amphitheatre – make Lucca memorable. The walls make it unique.

Lucca's walls are like no other. The city has been encircled four times. The Romans built the first wall and a stretch of it can still be seen in the Church of Santa Maria della Rosa. But the city outgrew that wall so they built another in the twelfth century, and then a third in the fifteenth century. Two centuries later they decided to do the job once and for all. It took them one hundred years, but the result is the most imposing city wall imaginable – pink, proud, perfect. It goes right round the city. It is wide, wooded, welcoming. It is a linear park, an unforgettable promenade.

It was intended of course as a fortification but the city has never been attacked since the wall was built – except by water. The wall saved Lucca from the great flood of 1812 which would so easily have swept away the whole city. When Elisa Bonaparte, who was out of town at the time, heard of the flood she rushed back. But in spite of her overtures, they would not risk opening her gate, the Elisa, even for her, so they hoisted her by crane over the wall.

Socially that was essential, for from that day to this, the inhabitants *Lucco dentro* (inside Lucca) have looked down on those *Lucca fuori* (outside Lucca). The walls define the inner circle.

October 1988

A Penny for
Your Thoughts
on the Guy

The two most famous dates in British history, one a year and one a day, are 1066 and November 5. Everyone knows them. But ask anyone the day on which the Battle of Hastings was fought or the year of the Gunpower plot and they will be struggling. It is not easy to light upon the date of the battle of Hastings. One version of The Anglo-Saxon Chronicle says: 'Count William came from Normandy to Pevensey on Michaelmas Eve and as soon as they were able to move on they built a castle at Hastings.' Michaelmas Eve is September 28, so we know when the Conqueror arrived, but when did he conquer? If you read on through the Chronicle you come to this sentence. 'The Battle took place on the festival of Calixtus the Pope.' And that, according to a learned footnote, was Saturday, October 14. So now you know.

The year of the Gunpowder Plot is no mystery. It was 1605 and therefore ought to be easy to remember, but then the warning jingle omits it.

'Remember, remember, the Fifth of November, Gunpowder, treason and plot,' it says, but makes no mention of the year. And how many people can remember the next two lines?

'There is no reason why Gunpowder treason should ever be forgot.'

Nor is there. Left to itself November in Britain may be a dull month with damp days and dark nights, but we make up for it by setting the place alight. Most families, certainly those with children, have a bonfire and fireworks or attend a public bonfire. The public events are increasingly at the weekend even if the Fifth falls in midweek, though it will not matter this year because Saturday is the Fifth.

But the remembrance is not what it was. November 5, no matter when it falls, ought to be made a public holiday. Parliament said so. It should, it said, be 'a holiday for ever in thankfulness to God for our deliverance'. And that came from the heart, for it is often forgotten that the Plot was not simply to blow up the Houses of Parliament, the buildings, but everyone inside – the Lords, the Commons AND the King. On November 5, 1605, King James the First of England and Sixth of Scotland attended Parliament in person to open the new session. Had the gunpowder in the vaults gone off, he would have departed too, and goodness knows what bloodshed would have followed. If kings not only had to be deposed but to be disposed of, Parliament preferred to do it itself, as James's son Charles the First was to discover – on January 30, 1649.

The Gunpowder Plot had been intended as a prelude to a Catholic rising, but one of the plotters – known to history as Treasonable Tresham – gave warning to his Catholic relative Lord Mounteagle, who gave the game away. The Yeoman of the Guard searched the cellars, discovered the gunpowder, and arrested among others the man who was to light the fuse – Guy Fawkes. He came to a very nasty end.

And yet if he is not a hero, no more is he a villain. The British, I suspect, have long had a sneaking feeling that he was not all bad. Blowing up the Houses of Parliament may not be within the constitution, but it does our legislators no harm to be reminded that it might have happened. It keeps them in their place. And certainly the British light bonfires for no other character in their history, and light fireworks on virtually no other day in the year.

Some towns go much further than bonfires and rockets. In Bridgewater, Somerset, they have a Guy Fawkes Carnival. It is a great torchlight procession with illuminated floats and thousands of squibs. In previous centuries it was known to get out of hand. The authorities decreed that it was far too riotous and appointed a municipal committee to keep it in order. At Harlington in Middlesex they have a Leg of Pork Supper, and have had ever since November 5, 1606. An unknown donor gave a parcel of land to the parish church in thanksgiving for the deliverance of King and Parliament and the income from the land pays for the Pork Supper which the bellringers enjoy – after they have rung the bells.

In Ottery St Mary in Devon they celebrate Bonfire Night by setting light to eight barrels of tar and rolling them down a hill into a crowd. It used to be considered very manly to catch a barrel. In Shebbear, which is also in Devon, they turn the Devil's Boulder. The church bells ring and then the villagers make their way to an old oak tree in the middle of the village. Under the tree is a huge stone – the Devil's Boulder. The villagers, panting and pushing, turn the stone and peace and prosperity in Shebbear are guaranteed for another year. In the city of York, where Guy Fawkes was born, they get up to mischief, not on November 5, but on the night before. It is known as Mischief Night but it too has been known to get out of hand, and may again.

Perhaps they were more prudent in the City of London where for more than three centuries they have settled for a sermon. In 1665, Theophilus Royle, a City draper, left money to pay for a Gunpowder Sermon in perpetuity to be preached at the Church of St Mary-le-Bow. He also left money for candles, though not for fireworks. Myself, I most enjoyed a Bonfire Night when I was above it all. I was in a plane flying from London to Manchester. It was a clear night, starry and cloudless. First over London, then over Birmingham, and finally over Manchester as we came in to land, I looked down on bonfires burning and fireworks erupting. It was a marvellous sight.

I also saw Manchester City playing under floodlights. They too look better from a few thousand feet.

November 1988

Questions for Christmas

I have spent a large part of the year in the Middle Ages, and I have felt very much at home. But then so did they. The twelve centuries between the conversion of Constantine and the death of Dante witnessed many horrors but they were times when mystery had not been reduced to quaintness and when logic and faith were not thought to be incompatible.

The people then did not know as much about the world as we do now, but they were more at home in it. They accepted the wholeness of living with all its dangers. They accepted that they were owned by life and did not control it. Not us. We lay claim to only part of living and by seeking to tame it often make it safe, but desolate. They put faith in God. We put our faith in everything except God.

We shake our heads over their devotions and then put up with the antics of the television evangelists in the United States. Why is it that for all the theological insight stored in the major traditions of Christians and for all the debate all over the world among thinking Christians, the lunacy and blasphemy of the more extreme electronic evangelists can still gain a sincere, if credulous, following. It can of course be comical. In Amarillo, Texas, you can come across filling stations bearing the message: 'Jesus Christ is King. Alternators started.'

But it can also be chilling. Many American fundamentalists are enthralled by the prospect of Armageddon. They believe that they are the terminal generation with a prospect of inevitable nuclear war. This will be, they say, the great tribulation forecast in the Book of Revelation. At the decisive moment, which is near, the true believers will be rescued and raptured into heaven. The rest of us, who do not share this folly, will live, burn, and

89

die horribly. Some of them have car stickers which say: 'In the case of rapture, this automobile may be left unmanned.'

And this kind of nonsense, which medieval scholars would have exposed and condemned, is catching. We are beginning to hear it over here. I had reason not so long ago to rebuke a young clergyman whose public utterances seemed to me to be in error and possibly in sin. My rebuke must have reached the ears of his parishioners because an elderly lady in his congregation wrote me a very moving letter. In it she said that the offending priest would not visit the sick nor pray for the dead. His services were all silly songs and American videos, and in five years he had reduced a thriving church into a hotbed of discontent and misery.

The fundamental flaw in many of the most popular and most thriving religious movements is that they speak of God as if He were created in our image and not we in His. God is not a credit card or a rabbit's foot. You do not ring Him up and ask a favour. Hot lines to heaven are all the rage at present, but it is as well to ask who is controlled and who controlling. Is the one who says he is through to God seeking guidance or power?

And why all this worship of the self? A fibre diet no doubt keeps you regular, but is it not disturbing that lessons of morality have only hit home because they happen to have coincided with the cult of the self, with all its sacramental procedures to ensure physical well being? People are changing the food they eat and the way they live not because of the Sermon on the Mount but because of admiration for Jane Fonda or fear of Aids.

It is not enough to base self-control on the small world of our own well-being. Our well-being belongs to the health of a larger world and is not simply the prerogative of the comfortable half of the world who do not have to react to hunger, homelessness and hopelessness every day. When are we, the comfortable ones, going to exercise our option for self-control not as part of an individual self-beautification scheme, but as an admission of the wholeness of life?

Loaves and fishes would strengthen many people on their journey through life, but they have to be distributed, a duty as unfulfilled as self-preservation is unfulfilling. I say strength for the journey, but perhaps we should aim for completeness, which

includes the weakness of lives on the threshold of completion –
the insights of the old.

There is a beautiful passage towards the end of Ecclesiastes
which describes the physical exhaustion, the fear and the frailty
of old age. When strong men stoop and are afraid to walk in the
street, their eyes grow dim and they can barely hear when the
dawn chorus wakes them. At this time, the writer of Ecclesiastes
says, the almond tree, the watching tree, whose name is like the
watchfulness of God, comes into flower. The beauty of God, he
says, which should be enough strength for any journey, has the
strength of fruit blossom, which will only bear fruit if it dies.
The end of our journey, will be its beginning. A poet in the
seventh century said it all in one verse.

Pilgrim remember,
For all your pain,
The Master you seek abroad
You will find at home –
Or walk in vain.

Happy Christmas.

December 1988

February, Such
a Blessed Month
in Britain

February is the month in Britain when people clear their throats, not because it is the month of bronchial infection, though there is a lot of it about, but because February is the month when throats are blessed. I discovered this about ten years ago. A friend with a sore throat rang me and asked in a whisper if I would stand in for him on an overseas service broadcast about Britain in February? 'What happens in Britain in February?' I asked. 'Not a lot,' he said and took himself off to bed.

But he was wrong. February, as I found out, is a blessed month in Britain. On February 3, which is St Blaise's Day, people with sore throats pop into St Ethelreda's Church in Ely Place in London – a lovely old church – to have their throats blessed. St Blaise was a bishop in Armenia in the fourth century. A boy was brought to him who was near the point of death because he had a fishbone stuck in his throat. Blaise removed the bone and the boy's mother was so grateful that when Blaise was imprisoned she brought him food and candles to his prison cell. Sore throats are now blessed at frequent intervals throughout his feast day.

At Berwick on Tweed in February they bless the salmon nets. Just before midnight on February 14 they hold a short open-air service. On the stroke of midnight the first net is cast into the River Tweed, and if that first net contains a salmon the fish is presented to the vicar.

At Blidworth in Nottinghamshire, they not only bless the

babies in February, they rock them in public. This rocking ceremony was all the rage in the Middle Ages. In every parish the baby boy baptised nearest to the date of Purification was presented in church in memory of the Presentation of the infant Jesus. He was rocked before the altar in a flower decked cradle and then carried in his cradle in procession through the village. At Blidworth, where the parish church is dedicated to St Mary of the Purification, they have revived the rocking ceremony. It takes place on the nearest Sunday every year to February 2. The baby is baptised in the morning then rocked in the afternoon. And is made to feel very important.

The February ceremony I most enjoy, though I have only seen it once, is the ceremony called Hurling the Silver Ball, which takes place at St Ives in Cornwall. It is rather like a game of Pass the Parcel. It starts at half past ten in the morning on the first Monday of the month at the parish church. The mayor throws into the crowd a silver ball, which is about the size of a tennis ball but made of wood and covered in silver leaf. The ball is then swiftly passed from hand to hand through a great multitude of children and grown-ups filling the streets and the seashore. Whoever holds the ball at the stroke of midday has to take it back to the mayor in the Guildhall. In return the winner gets a prize. Twenty five pence.

Sir John Cass would not have thought much of that. Sir John was a sheriff of London who founded a school in 1709 which is named after him. On the day on which he sat down to make his will – with the intention of leaving everything to the school – he died at his desk of a haemorrhage before he could sign his name.

Every year, on February 20, a service is held in St Botolph's Church in Aldgate in his name. The children from his school attend the Sir John Cass Service wearing, in their hats and lapels, red feather quills in memory of his blood-stained pen.

If Easter falls early, as it does this year, February is enriched by Shrove Tuesday, Pancake Tuesday. Two places vie with each other in Britain to stage the best pancake race. At eleven o'clock in the morning at Margate in Kent every woman living or working within the town is invited to run a distance of three hundred yards along St Mildred's Road to the Bridge Hotel.

They race carrying a pancake in a frying pan. They have to

bring their own frying pans but the pancakes are provided, and the winner gets an engraved copper plated frying pan.

The Margate pancake race is a fine event but it is not quite in the same class as the Olney pancake race. This is the Derby of pudding races. The pancake race at Olney, in Buckinghamshire, has been run every year since 1445. Competitors must be women of the parish over the age of sixteen. They must wear an apron and a head covering – a bonnet or a headsquare.

With a toss of their pancakes the women dash from the market place to the parish church, where the winner receives a kiss from the bell ringer. The Olney race is international now because it is run in competition with a race in the town of Liberal in Kansas.

The ringing of the church bell at noon is the traditional start to pancake making on Shrove Tuesday in many villages in Britain. And at Scarborough, the seaside resort on the Yorkshire coast, the pancake bell which was once hung and rung in a hospital is now housed in the town museum. But it is still solemnly rung at noon every Shrove Tuesday. Yorkshire people will tell you that they make the best pancakes. But so they should; they get plenty of practice. What are pancakes but Yorkshire pudding with sugar added?

The best entertainment of all on Shrove Tuesday in Britain is at Ashbourne in Derbyshire, where Isaak Walton used to buy his tackle on his way to fish in Dovedale. Ashbourne is divided by a stream called Henore Brook, and that stream divides the town every bit as much as a railway track or a great river. Those Up'ards and those Down'ards of the brook are great rivals.

That rivalry bursts forth on Shrove Tuesday. After the Pancake bell has tolled at midday and the housewives have cooked their pancakes and their families have eaten their fill, the townspeople gather in Shaw Croft, a field in the middle of the town. They sing Auld Lang Syne and God Save the Queen and then the Shrovetide football match begins. A specially made, decorated, ball is carried into the centre of the field by some distinguished visitor to the town, who is carried by two strong men. He tosses the ball into the air. After that anything goes.

Any number of men can join in as long as they indicate whether they are playing Up'ards or Down'ards. The goals are three miles apart, and as the play rages to and fro, the players are free to kick, carry, or hurl the ball. They also tend to kick, carry, or hurl each other. Play begins at two in the afternoon and has been known to continue until ten o'clock at night. Neither sleet nor snow discourages the players, and one year a group of men pursued the ball through a fishpond breaking the ice as they pushed forward. It is usually impossible to tell who has won.

All this I reported to my overseas listeners. My silent friend thanked me, when he got his voice back, and now he makes a point of popping into St Ethelreda's Church on Saint Blaise's Day.

January/February 1989

A Harmless
Superstition

I t was not until I became the editor of an evening paper that I discovered what a hold over people horoscopes have. One day, by accident not intent, the horoscope failed to appear in the paper and the phones were soon alight with calls from distraught newsagents. 'The readers are in revolt,' said one.

And they were. When questioned they said that their day was incomplete without the stars, but when questioned further they admitted they could not remember a word of their horoscope ten minutes after they had read it. All of which confirmed my view that a horoscope is a harmless superstition and no one in their right mind should take it seriously. But I never omitted it again.

It came, I remember, from California – where else? I bought the first English rights and the editor of a neighbouring evening paper bought the second rights. This meant that I published it a day before him, so, as I pointed out at the time, if you had a good day you could have it twice by changing your paper.

I lost faith in that particular forecaster when, during the postal strike, I noticed that the forecast for Capricorn (i.e. me) said, 'Expect a letter today.' I decided I could not go on misleading the readers so for the next fortnight, until I found a new astrologer, I wrote the daily horoscopes myself, promising the readers happiness and bliss provided they loved their neighbours, though not their neighbours' wives.

It is many years now since I gave up editing an evening paper and I had not looked at a horoscope since (not even when it was revealed that Mrs Reagan relied upon a Californian astrologer) until the beginning of this year. I was reading various people's forecasts for 1989 – politicians, economists, columnists and the like, strengthened by the thought that none of them could be as wildly wrong as the Treasury's forecasts, when I hit upon the prophecy of a soothsayer. The world, he said, will be turned upside down in March.

I was reading this in midwinter. The witch hazel was already in flower in the garden. The day was mild, but the news bulletins spoke of snow in Las Vegas, and, even more astonishing, in Damascus. Imagine if Paul had set off for Damascus and been turned back because of the snow, the history of Christianity would have been different.

The world *is* upside down, I thought, further provoked by a Trog cartoon inspired by the headline 'UK's warmest New Year ever', which had a man saying, 'Why doesn't the greenhouse effect ever work in summer?'

But why March in particular, I thought? Then it dawned on me. March is always an odd month, and nowhere odder than at Lanark Cross in Scotland, where they celebrate the start of March with a happening called Whuppity Scoorie. At six o'clock in the evening on March 1 the children gather at the parish church, armed with balls of tightly packed paper each on the end of a piece of string.

As the church bells begin to peal the children race three times round the church whirling their paper balls – called their maces – round their heads, trying to knock each other off their stride. The one who outruns the others, reaching the church door first is declared the winner, and receives a lump sum of money. The others scramble for pennies thrown to them.

Why do they do it? Because, long ago, in a battle between the English and the Scots, an English soldier sought sanctuary in the parish church of Lanark Cross. The doors were shut and he ran three times round the church shouting, 'Sanctuary' – Scoorie. His Scots pursuers chased him crying, 'Up at ye' – Whuppity. The church doors opened and the soldier took refuge there.

Only one thing still puzzles me about Whuppity Scoorie. Why should the Scots celebrate an English escape? And why on St David's Day?

Perhaps the March Hare knows the answer. He is the symbol of the madness of that month. It is, for instance, the only month in which a game of rugby begins four weeks after the ball has been thrown into play. This too is in Scotland, at Jedburgh.

On Candlemas Day, February 2, a rugby ball is thrown in the

air. Then everyone goes home. They return in March to play the Ba' game. There are no rules. Two sides take part – the Uppies and the Downies. There is no limit on numbers or size and there is no referee. The small boys of the town have a game of their own from noon until two, and then the men take over and battle until sundown.

They take it seriously, but not as seriously as the Welsh take their rugby. In Wales in March in any pub near any rugby ground somebody will always tell a stranger the story of the local man who scored the winning try against the English team at Twickenham. The try was suspect. The man himself always had a nagging doubt that he had not grounded the ball after he crossed the line.

He died after a long and otherwise virtuous life and went to heaven. The saint on the gate inquired if he had anything on his conscience which might debar him from paradise. 'Well,' he said, 'I have. I scored the winning try for Wales against England at Twickenham in 1908 but I have always wondered if I really touched the ball down.'

'Oh, you did, you did,' said the saint. 'I was watching from above. You grounded the ball fairly and squarely. Come on in.' The old rugby player was much relieved. 'Thank you, St Peter,' he said. 'I'm not St Peter,' said the saint. 'I'm St David.'

March 1989

May Day
Alert

M ay Day is a Monday this year. It is the first time for eleven
years that May 1 has fallen on a Monday. The last time it
happened was the first time that May Day was a public holiday.
Do you remember how puzzled everyone was? What will we do
with it, we said? Not a lot, was the answer.

Practically every other nation in Europe – France, Germany,
Italy, Spain, Portugal and the Scandinavian countries – has long
taken May Day off, and in Eastern European countries it is
almost compulsory to be seen to celebrate. Nor have we ever
been short of May Day celebrations. Traditionally the day is
marked by games and sports, particularly archery and Morris
dancing and the setting up of the Maypole to dance round. Robin
Hood claimed the day as his own and he and Maid Marion were
dubbed Lord and Lady of the May. May Day was also traditionally the day of the Festival of the London chimney sweeps.

But over the years, precisely because May 1 was not an official
public holiday, the May festivities were kept for the first Saturday
in May. Countless towns and villages in England elect a May
Queen, dress her in flowers and finery, and carry her in
procession through the streets. My favourite is the Royal May
Day Festival at Knutsford in Cheshire, Mrs Gaskell's *Cranford*.

In 1978 May Festival organisers throughout the country
agonised over whether to change their date from the first
Saturday to the first day of the month, now that it was an official
holiday, and as it happened, a Monday. But most of them
decided to wait a year to see what happened, and what happened,
of course, was that in 1979 the bank holiday was not on the first
of the month but on the first Monday of the month, which was

May 7. So almost everybody stuck to the first Saturday, May 5, for their festivities and the Monday was something of a flop.

It has never recovered. Of all our bank holidays it is the one that matters least. People are still puzzled why we have it. You hear them say: I thought it was at the end of the month. They are referring to the Spring Bank Holiday which is the last Monday of May. This year the two holidays are four weeks apart. Next year they will be three weeks apart. And neither this year nor next will Whit Monday be either of them. It never is. I have argued before, both here and elsewhere, that we have made a mess of May. We ought to cancel both the May bank holidays and celebrate Whitsun instead. And if we need another holiday we should celebrate Ascension Day. It is always a Thursday, forty days after Easter and ten days before Whit Sunday. And it is the day for beating the bounds.

This annual circumlocution of a town's boundaries is particularly popular in the border country and one of the best examples is at Berwick-on-Tweed. But they also do it at the Tower of London, not every year, but every third year, so you will have to wait until next year to see it. The Yeoman Warders, in full dress uniform, walk round the Tower, pausing at every 31st boundary stone and say:

'Cursed is he who removeth his neighbour's land mark . . .'
and then,

'Whack it boys, whack it.'

It is not to be missed.

If you are stuck for something to do on Whit Sunday, May 14 this year, go to Bristol and to the most beautiful church in the city, St Mary Redcliffe. It was on Whit Sunday 1468 that William Canynges, the great merchant prince of Bristol who gave up all his worldly goods to become a priest, celebrated Holy Communion for the first time in St Mary Redcliffe. Accordingly, every Whit Sunday a great civic service is held in the church. The Lord Mayor and the Corporation come. The church is strewn with rushes. The worshippers carry posies. And they call the day not Whit Sunday, but Rush Sunday.

On Rush Monday, on the other side of England at St Ives in Huntingdon, there is another ceremony endowed by legacy. It is known as Dicing for Bibles. One Dr Robert Wilde left money in his will in 1678, and at noon every Whit Monday the children from the local Sunday School throw dice to see who can win one of a dozen bibles diced for every year. Which is another good reason for restoring the Whitsun bank holiday.

A final thought. A few years ago I went all the way to the village of Ipplepen in Devon because I had been told that there they not only beat the bounds but bump them. Young and old, fortified with plenty of cider, are seized by the arms and legs and bounced up and down as they are dragged through fields and streams, hedges and ditches. But when I got there I found that they only do it every forty years or so. They did it in 1910 and again in 1950. Will they bump again in 1990?

Answers on a postcard please.

April 1989

101

Olympics in Manchester

The next Olympic Games, in 1992, will be in Barcelona. The ones after that, in 1996, are open to offers. Manchester is Britain's choice. I have had a hand in Manchester's Olympic bid from the beginning and have been greatly occupied in working out how best to present the case.

I argued recently that any country which is not knee-deep in insurrection can present a plausible case for *wanting* the Olympic Games. It is good publicity. It is good business. It is good international relations. And all these are compelling arguments, but they are largely irrelevant. What matters is not what a country wants or gains, but what the Olympic Games need and get.

I believe that ideally the Olympic Games need four things – the freedom of an open society, the support of a prosperous society, the convenience of an internationally understood language, and the friendship of a people for whom sport is a universal pastime. On all those counts, Britain qualifies. For this country the Olympic Games is not a prize to be won but a Festival to be enjoyed. The competitors win the prizes and the country gets the pleasure, which it then shares with the world.

Britain, I am sure, and not every country can make this claim, can offer the Olympic Games efficiency without officiousness, organisation without harassment, and support without prejudice. It wants the competitors to enjoy themselves, and it has the flair and the capacity to make that happen.

That, when I am pressed, is my sales pitch. But why Manchester? And why 1996? The first modern Olympic Games was in 1896 and it was held in Athens, so it is no surprise that Athens wants to stage the centenary games in 1996. But it so happens that 1896 was an important date for Manchester too. That year saw the official opening of a great man-made waterway from Manchester to the sea, deep enough and wide enough to turn a city 40 miles inland into a great industrial port.

That waterway was the Manchester Ship Canal, and now 100 years later the Ship Canal is being offered both as the location and as the inspiration of the 1996 Olympic Games. The plan is to build along the banks of the Canal, whose waters once reflected the activities of the greatest concentration of industry in the world, the greatest concentration of sports arenas in the world. There will be a new Olympic stadium, a new Olympic velodrome, a new Olympic pool, a new Olympic village, a new Olympic city – all designed by computer in the city which built the first computer in the world.

Already, all along the banks of the Ship Canal and the River Mersey, from Salford Quays to Albert Dock, the next century is taking shape. The North West of England, which was *the* place of the past, is not visibly, as we show every Olympic visitor, the place of the future.

Every member of the Manchester Olympic Committee can tick off the assets: the North West is easy to get to; it has two international airports, one of them the fastest growing airport in Europe; it is better served by motorways than anywhere else in Britain; it has more hotel beds than the whole of Los Angeles; it has no fewer than five universities and a dozen other residential colleges of higher education; it has nine theatres, two dozen museums and galleries and three symphony orchestras.

It has more people who play sport than anywhere else in Britain, and more people who watch sport than anywhere else in Britain. It has, we tell anyone who asks, the vision, the structure, and the intention of staging an Olympic Games which would not only delight the competitors and the world, but would also stimulate the regeneration of a proud region of Britain on the brink of a new century.

And that, we believe, is an Olympic ideal. The Princess Royal, who is President of the British Olympic Association agrees and believes that Manchester's bid has every chance of success. She has said so publicly.

The doubters say that, if only for sentimental reasons, Athens will get the Games in 1996, China in 2000, somewhere on the

American continent in 2004, and Manchester must wait until 2008. That would be symmetry they say, because Britain staged the Olympics in 1908 and again in 1948.

But I don't want to wait 21 years. After all, I might not be here. Seven years will be quite long enough.

May 1989

Publishers' note: Brian Redhead was indefatigable in his support for Manchester's Olympic bids for 1996 and 2000.

Common but Kissable

June is a right royal month in Britain. It is the month when the principal sporting events are blessed either by a royal presence or by a royal title, or by both.

It is also the month of the Queen's official birthday, and the month when Her Majesty makes herself apparent to her people. The great event is the annual parade to celebrate her birthday, the ceremony we know as Trooping the Colour.

Today the ceremony is a spectacle, but there was a time when it was a crucial preparation for battle. In the days before 'mercenary' became a dirty word, most armies included large contingents of foreign troops rented for the occasion.

It was of such a contingent of hired hands that the Duke of Wellington made his famous observation: 'I don't know what effect these men will have upon the enemy, but by God they frighten me.'

To make sure they not only frightened but fought the enemy, the colour was trooped before them. They were shown the flag they had to follow on the battlefield, to make sure they fought for the side that was paying them.

The Trooping the Colour ceremony now always takes place at eleven o'clock on a Saturday morning in June in Horse Guards Parade in Whitehall. This year it is on Saturday June 17. And the world will watch the Queen as she rides to and from Buckingham Palace.

Her Majesty has more than one palace, but only one castle – Windsor. William the Conqueror began the building of it. Henry I was the first to hold court in it. And Edward III spent a fortune on it. Edward also founded the Order of the Garter, so it is only right that the annual procession of the Knights of the Garter should take place at Windsor Castle. And this year it will be on Monday, June 19.

The Most Noble Order of the Garter is the highest order of knighthood in the kingdom. Legend has it that it was founded by Edward in 1348, when the Countess of Salisbury accidentally dropped her garter at a court ball. The King picked it up and seeing the sniggering glances of the spectators rebuked them for their indelicate thoughts by binding the blue ribbon round his own knee, saying: *Honi Soit Qui Mal Y Pense* (Evil to him who evil thinks).

The courtiers were probably right to think the worst because Edward's was a bawdy court. After his success in battle against both the Scots and the French, he devoted his life to pleasure. And although England was stricken with bubonic plague – the Black Death – he had almost every carpenter and stone mason in the land pressed into working at Windsor.

Historians have called Edward's Windsor the 'Versailles of the fourteeth century', but Edward and his knights saw themselves as the true descendants of King Arthur and the Knights of the Round Table.

And although the Knights of the Garter saw their order as an order of chivalry, it did not inhibit their roistering. Indeed Henry, Earl of Derby and Duke of Lancaster, and the King's greatest crony, wrote a book in which he confessed that he had often drunk so much with his noble companions that his legs would not carry him to bed. He also wrote that he preferred to kiss common women rather than noble women because common women responded more enthusiastically.

Today the Garter ceremony is sober and dignified with everyone on their best behaviour, but the habits and the insignia, the costumes and the decorations, are magnificent.

And the procession from Windsor Castle to St George's Chapel, a fine church within the castle walls, of the twenty-five Knights of the Order led by the Queen as Sovereign is one of the summer joys of Britain in June.

But it is more than that. When people, as they do, make mock of such ceremonies or dismiss them as of no importance, I always quote the words of Natalya Solzhenitsyn. She is the wife of Alexander Solzhenitsyn, the Russian novelist. She was in

London a few years ago and was watching the Changing of the Guard at Buckingham Palace from a hotel window.

When the ceremony was over she turned and said to her companions: 'I knew in London you had the Change of the Guard, but I did not know that it happened so naturally. Tradition is one of the joys of England and it is something which cannot be bought or sold. It is the feet of a nation. Without it, it has no legs and cannot stand.'

June 1989

Summertime Views

S ometimes I think that there are only eleven months in a year. We have taken to lumping together July and August. For evidence of this, you have only to look at the front cover of this magazine.

But July and August used to be very different. July was the month when people came together. It was the great month for gatherings. August was the month when they went away. The numbers assembling in any one place may have been similar, but the motives were different. In August people went somewhere else; in July they celebrated at home. I think it is still like that. July is the month for marquees on the lawn and strawberry teas, for top hats and tails at Buckingham Palace.

August is the month when Britain is on holiday. The schools are closed; Parliament is silent; offices are empty; hotels full. Given the choice, everybody says that he or she would choose another month to go away, when prices are lower and the weather is better, but in truth those who work in August always look as if they wish they were on holiday.

July is essentially the prelude to that holiday. Much more than December it completes the working year. Then everything starts again in September. People come together in July in the fellowship of their calling, to commemorate what they have been up to.

It is the month of the country show, the month when the growers and the breeders, the farmers and the gardeners, gather in some prize place to demonstrate their achievement. At one time there was even one country show in an inner city – the Manchester Show.

The country came to that inner city in July when the marquees went up in Platt Fields, barely a mile from the city centre. The Manchester Show was a civic show, a matter of municipal pride. It began as a flower show and grew. Soon it had everything that was not urban – flowers and fruit, livestock and game, fish and fowl. And for three days the citizens enjoyed themselves like country people, as if there were no inner city problems, no slums, no vandalism, no violence on the streets. Then they went on holiday. Sadly the city, or more precisely the city fathers, have lost interest in the Manchester Show, and there will not be one this year.

Even with mines closed and employment severely reduced, the Durham Miners have not given up their July Show, the Miners' Gala (pronounced Gayla, nor Garla). It will be held in Durham City this year as usual, a compulsory event for Labour leaders, no Tories allowed.

Someone should have invited Mr Gorbachev, and then they could have told him about Chopwell, the Durham mining village which during the General Strike of 1926 declared itself the capital of the first Soviet in Britain. A young man on a bike denied entrance to the village at the time demanded to to taken to the commissar. They still laugh about it.

Come August many will be on holiday, and not all of them abroad. There was a time when almost everybody went to the seaside crowding into local resorts in such numbers that small boys used to calculate that if every inhabitant of Britain stood at the same August moment at the water's edge in a ring around the coastline, they could all hold hands. And even today half the inhabitants of industrial Britain take their holidays at home – by which I mean away but not abroad.

Ten million go to Blackpool which is still the premier seaside resort in Britain. Blackpool does everything to excess. Its promenades are longer, its piers stronger, its beach wider, its big dipper dippier than in any other resort in Britain, if not in the world.

Blackpool thinks big in a way which is quite out of character in Britain. There is nothing quietly superior about the place. It is brashly the biggest. Genteel people cower from its clamour, but for many for whom the purpose of a holiday is not to get away from it all but to have a good time together, Blackpool is still the first choice.

It is a citadel of mass entertainment. Rain or shine – and Blackpool has one of the best sunshine records in Britain – there is no danger of having nothing to do. The secret of its continuing appeal is that it keeps all the old pleasures and adds to them all the new. You can still dance to the organ in the Tower Ballroom and then see Cats at the Opera House.

August in Britain is a glorious month, but then glorious is a very English word. Queen Elizabeth the First was Gloriana. The bloodless constitutional change of 1688 was the Glorious Revolution. The poet Dryden was Glorious John. English lawyers toast the Glorious Uncertainty of the Law, which has grown more uncertain this year with the coming of Lord Mackay of Clashfern. And August 12 is the Glorious Twelfth. It celebrates no past event but simply marks the beginning of the shooting season.

Roll on September.

July/August 1989

The Longest Day

Friday, September 1, 1939, was the longest day of my childhood. Fifteen years later, with the memory of it still fresh, I wrote about that day. Fifty years later, I can still remember every moment of it. And I am not alone. I was invited recently to judge a competition of essays recalling that first day of evacuation. I was all for giving a prize to every entry because they all revealed the same intense recollection.

There was never another day quite like it. Some had happy, some painful memories, but implicit in all the essays, and explicit in a few including the winning entry, was the question: why did no one dispute the decision to pack us all off to the country and to separate us from our families? Why did we go quietly?

The Government had expected a rebellion. Its intention was that all schoolchildren and all mothers with children under five, were to be moved that day from evacuation areas (the cities) to reception areas (the country). The plan was made known very hesitantly for fear of causing alarm. The Government had a terrified vision of panic-stricken mobs fleeing from the great cities on the outbreak of war. They envisaged using troops to master the crowds and actually called in a former Indian Army officer to advise on the handling of crowds out of control.

Because of the Government's dithering the lists of those to be evacuated remained sadly incomplete. Only a third of the mothers with children under five registered. In London, only 69 per cent of schoolchildren were registered. In Sheffield, only 15 per cent. Newcastle-upon-Tyne and Gateshead did best with 80 per cent, four out of five, and I was one of them.

We did not go until after lunch, or after dinner as we put it. It was a sunny morning and we heard on the wireless that Hitler had invaded Poland. My friend Billy and I were quite sure that there was going to be a war. So was an old lady around the corner, who promptly put on her gas mask and went shopping wearing it. Billy and I nailed a picture of Hitler to the quarry fence and threw kitchen knives at it, adding to our indictment with every wild throw: 'That's for Austria,' we shouted, 'And that's for Czechoslovakia.' For nine-year-olds we were well informed. And then we ran down the street to sing a jingoistic jingle about Billy's brother, a handsome Territorial who was killed not many months later.

Everyone was friendly. Other mothers in the street who usually shrank from our rowdy presence embraced us repeatedly and gave us things to eat, fearing perhaps that it would have to last us for the duration. A brother and sister in the street who were at different schools, and therefore were to be evacuated to different places, staged an elaborate charade of parting, with mock tears – though one or two of those watching wept in earnest. At last, around two o'clock in the afternoon with our new rucksacks on our backs, we went to school, where we were sorted and labelled and put in line. We then marched to Scotswood station.

A few mothers came to wave us off, but if they were hoping for a tearful farewell, they were disappointed. Once in the train we were all immediately too busy eating to wave goodbye. It was a strange journey for us, not so much because we were going to an unknown destination, but because the teacher was so amiable. Until then we had never known him speak kindly, but perhaps he too realised that school was never going to be the same again. And he became a friend. He entertained us with tricks with matches and blew smoke rings, while we squirted each other with orange juice and queued for the lavatory. Then we became restless and were to stay restless.

The train ended its journey at Dalston on the other side of Carlisle, and there we stood on the platform for what seemed like hours while they decided what to do with us. Eventually they marched us to a nearby school and gave us our iron rations: a carrier bag each of canned food. The bags weighed almost as much as we did, but they did not include a can-opener, though Billy found that the implement on his pocket knife for removing stones from horses' hooves worked just as well and he and I tucked in as we waited.

We were divided into bus-loads, one for each village which was to house us. There were screaming rows as families were separated and then reunited. It was almost midnight when we reached our destination, a village our train had passed through many hours earlier. By this time we really looked like inner-city children – pale, weary, querulous.

The villagers had gathered in the school hall to greet us. They looked like farmers at a disappointing auction. They made their bids reluctantly though, to be fair, no one actually prodded us with a walking stick. After half an hour, Billy and I were the only two not chosen. 'It looks,' said the village postmaster and baker, 'as if I shall have to take that cheeky pair.'

He took us and we walked up the village street in the pitch dark. There were no street lights, and no lights from the houses either because the black-out had already been imposed. I can still hear every step we took. It was well into the early hours when we finally went to bed and even then we spent quite a time testing the springs of the mattress.

For one reason or another Billy and I left the post office after three weeks and were separated. But not before the postmaster had sold our iron rations in his shop.

September 1989

Time to
Take Stock

October is a divided month. It is a favourite month for elections, for party conferences, for rallies of all kinds in favour of one cause and against another. But it is not the political divisions which I have in mind. It is something much more fundamental than that. It is the division between summer and winter, or more precisely between summer time and winter time.

To make sure that everyone is aware of this division, of that change from summer time to winter time, everyone has an extra hour in bed. This is made possible because October is the only month in the year which includes a 25-hour day, the day on which the clock is put back an hour.

Back, I would argue, to where it belongs. The clock is put forward one hour in March so that people may make fuller use of the daylight hours. By advancing the clock one hour, there is one less hour of daylight before people get up in the morning, and one more hour while they are up.

The idea of 'daylight saving' was first put forward by Benjamin Franklin, the American inventor, but it was William Willett, a Chelsea builder, who campaigned for it. It was first adopted by the Germans as a wartime measure in 1916, and Britain hastily followed. From then on we had Greenwich Mean Time in the winter, and in the summer British Summer Time which was one hour in advance.

Between World Wars One and Two, British Summer Time started on the day following the third Saturday in April (unless that was Easter Day in which case it started on the day following the second Saturday in April). It ended on the day following the first Saturday in October.

114

But during World War Two, to 'save' even more daylight hours, we had Summer Time throughout the winter, and Double Summer Time throughout the summer. This meant that we were two hours ahead of Greenwich and the midsummer evenings were light almost until midnight.

We celebrated victory against the Germans in 1945 by reverting to Greenwich Mean Time in winter and to British Summer Time in summer. But in 1947 because of the fuel crisis we had a summer of Double Summer Time. In 1961 Summer Time was extended by six weeks, beginning in March and ending at the end of October, on the day after the last Saturday.

And then on February 18, 1968, the clocks were advanced one hour and it was officially announced that from then on British Summer Time would be permanent. There was to be no putting the clocks back in October any more. British Summer Time was from now on to be British Standard Time, year in and year out.

It did not last. Come the winter, it was too dark in the mornings. The cows would not wake up to be milked. The farmers grumbled. They claimed never to see the sun in Scotland. And when two children were knocked down by a car in the dark of one gloomy morning as they made their way to school, the politicians surrendered.

The clocks went back one hour the next October, as they have done every October since, and everyone slept more easily in their beds. But there is once again disturbing talk. To coincide with the coming of the Single European Market in 1992, there are those who argue that Britain should fall in step with Europe which is one hour ahead of us both in winter and in summer.

That would mean either the restoration of the wartime diary of Summer Time and Double Summer Time, or – if the rest of Europe could be persuaded – the restoration of British Standard Time the year round.

I am all for Standard Time but not for BST. Standard Time or Zone Time, as it is sometimes called, is the system of timekeeping accepted in most parts of the world. It is based on twenty-four meridians, each fifteen degrees apart, starting from Greenwich. This gives an exact difference of an hour between any two adjacent zones.

It was, incidentally, first adopted by the railway companies in America in 1883 to overcome the obvious inconveniences caused by the differing local times on their routes. Standard Time is the sun's time, and when it is noon over Greenwich it should be noon over Britain.

If the hour is incovenient, the timetable, not the time should be changed. Get up an hour earlier in the summer months or an hour later in the winter. Start work at eight instead of nine or knock off at four instead of five. But keep the clock as it is. I get up most mornings at half-past four, summer and winter alike. I call that BST – Brian's Standard Time.

October 1989

Pageantry and
Pantomime

Never mind the Last Night of the Proms, come to the Last Night of the Street, said the voice on the phone. So I did. It was an invitation to a party in a pub to celebrate the departure of the last newspaper from Fleet Street. And it was a night of great nostalgia.

We talked about the editors we had known and feared, the colleagues we had admired, the politicians we had lampooned, and the eccentrics we missed. My favourite was the political columnist on a Sunday paper who lived in a beach hut in Marrakesh. He began his piece every week with the words, 'Here in Westminster . . .' and rarely if ever set foot in the place.

In a final gesture of farewell we moved from one pub to another and on the way I noticed for the first time the name of an alleyway, which I must have passed countless times before. It is called Turnagain Street.

The name, which if not unique is certainly very rare, refers (as you will have deduced) to the man who turned again – Dick Whittington. And that in turn provoked a great discussion. Would Dick Whittington figure in Mrs Thatcher's new history curriculum?

None of us could remember who first told us about him. We all had a rough idea of the story. Dick was an orphan boy who set off to London with his cat because he had been assured that the streets were paved with gold.

But when the pair of them got to London they found that the streets were not paved with gold and the people were very unfriendly. They were about to slink away when Bow Bells, the bells of the Church of St Mary the Bow, rang out their carillon which to Dick's ear and the cat's seemed to say:

Turn again Dick Whittington, Thrice Lord Mayor of London. So Dick turned again, back towards London, where he made his fortune and became thrice Lord Mayor.

That was the sum of our knowledge except for one among us, a city editor, who set out to explain that Dick Whittington was a hero of the market economy and bound to get into the new curriculum.

It was not true, he said, as legend had it, that Dick sold his cat for an enormous sum to the King of Barbary who was plagued with rats and mice, though he could see that that made a good story.

The truth was more monetary. Dick was a mercer who married well. He traded in coals brought to London in cats (a type of sailing ship). He traded at a profit and in those days the French word for such a purchase was *achat*. Hence Dick Whittington and his cat.

I prefer the panto story, said the theatre critic in our midst, and went on with considerable conviction to argue the case that Dick Whittington is the best of all parts for a principal boy. And that none had played it better than Dorothy Ward.

But the oldest among us said he could see no conflict between the legend, the truth and the panto. They were all enacted annually in the City of London.

Every year since 1215, when King John was on the throne, a new Lord Mayor of London is elected. At noon on the second Friday in November in Guildhall the retiring Lord Mayor hands over the insignia of office to the Lord Mayor elect. The ceremony is a pantomime in the strictest sense of the word because at the moment of handover no words are spoken. The ceremony is known as the Silent Change. What is more, he said, scarcely anyone can ever remember the name of the last Lord Mayor or the next, but everyone remembers Dick Whittington.

That set us all going again. Why is it, asked a literary critic, that some characters in history, who were real people, achieve the fame of fiction? He preferred Robin Hood as the best example. There was then an argument about whether Robin Hood was a real person. His adventures have been variously assigned from the reign of Richard I to that of Edward I and he could not have lived that long.

I blame the ballad writers, said one sub-editor, while the

118

theatre critic revised his judgement and said that Robin Hood was a good part for a principal boy also, and that Dorothy Ward had been good in that too.

But the sub-editor was right. When a character is taken up by the writer, whether of a great play or of a nursery rhyme, he or she is universally acknowledged. And becomes everybody's property.

I thought of a very good example on my way back to the Barbican that night. I was walking up Aldersgate Street along which Henry V led his troops in triumph after his victory at Agincourt. Would we think as highly of him, I thought, if Shakespeare had not written his play about him?

But then I remembered Hamlet and Lear. Are not they even better known?

November/December 1989

The Festival We All Forgot

Twelfth Night is not the night it once was. In one sense, of course, it never was a night. It is an Eve, the eve of the Twelfth Day of Christmas. The Twelfth Day, January 6, is the Feast of the Epiphany, the day upon which the infant Jesus was shown to the Three Wise Men.

The night before, January 5, used to be a riot, a wild night of merrymaking in England, to match anything seen in Scotland on New Year's Eve, and far in excess of any Christmas Eve celebrations. But not now. It may witness an office party for those who were too late to book a place for the week before or the week after Christmas.

It often heralds the start of the January sales in the shops. It is the night on which tidy-minded people remind themselves that they must take down the Christmas decorations tomorrow. But no one now wins the bean in the cake. At least, no one I have ever met.

There was a time, or so I am told, when they baked a Twelfth Night cake in almost every village in England. It was like a Christmas cake, filled with fruit and nuts, but in it they also put a bean. The small boy who got the slice of cake containing the bean was declared king, and he then played the part of the King in a charade.

To this day, there are people who say, when someone wins a prize in a lottery or a raffle: you have won the bean in the cake.

Twelfth Night was originally a pagan festival, and it is interesting that by the old Julian Calendar Christmas Day was on January 6. The Julian Calender was instituted by Julius Caesar himself in 46BC, so it looks as if the early Christians deliberately chose an important pagan day to celebrate the birth of Christ.

When Pope Gregory XIII corrected the calendar in 1582, Queen Elizabeth I, who was on the throne of England at the time, would not hear of it. She struck to the old calendar and must have been delighted when Shakespeare wrote Twelfth Night in 1600.

But now the play's the thing and the day, or rather the night, is forgotten. Perhaps it is because New Year's Eve has swept south and no one could contemplate two such merry nights in less than a week.

There are still villages in England where they celebrate plough Monday, which is the first Monday after January 6, in other words the first Monday after the Twelve Days of Christmas. They drag a plough through the village asking for plough money – not to spend on seed but on drink. God speed the plough, they say.

The best place to spend Plough Monday, they claim, is the village of Goathland, near Whitby in Yorkshire. Three sets of dancers – two adult and one of schoolboys – dance through the streets dressed in blue and pink uniforms and carrying swords with 30-inch blades. But the merriest place of all in England in January must be Haxey in Lincolnshire, where on the Twelfth Day, not the Twelfth Night, they compete for the Hood.

The story has it that on a January 6 sometime in the thirteenth century the Lady of the Manor, Lady de Mowbray, was blown away by the wind. Twelve labourers retrieved her, and she was so grateful and amused that she donated a piece of land, now known as the Hoodlands, to the villagers with the instruction that the rent from the land was to pay for a leather hood which the villagers would compete for annually.

They still do. In a game which looks not unlike American football, the villagers, dressed in colourful costumes and bearing such names as the King and the Fool and Boggans, fight for a hood. It is every man for himself and he who gets the hood and carries it successfully to the inn can drink his fill on the house.

I was explaining all this to a Scotsman, who was very scornful. That, he said, is nothing. Do you know that in Shetland they celebrate not the Twelve Days of Christmas but the Twenty-Four Days? And the Twenty-Fourth Night, the last night of the

121

Yule Festival is called Up-Helly-Aaa, meaning the upending of the holy days.

Though even that, he argued, was not to be compared to Burns Night, for that too, of course, falls in January, the 25, the anniversary of the birthday of Robert Burns.

I have only been to a proper Burns Supper once, but I found it a delicious feast in every sense – from the first bite of an Arbroath smokie, through the haggis and neeps, to the final dram; and from the first note of the pibroch to the final words of the Ode to the great chieftain of the pudding race.

You English should do that for Shakespeare on Twelfth Night, said my Scottish friend, adding that there is no point in waiting for his birthday because that is St George's Day and you never make much of that.

He had a point. We all have Christmas and New Year. But the Scots have Burns Night, the Welsh St David's Day, the Irish St Patrick's Day and the Americans Thanksgiving. England needs a festival of its own, so why not Twelfth Night?

After all, we already have the script.

January 1990

Can This
Be Us?

The trouble with this country, said the principal speaker at the meeting, is that we have fallen behind our competitors. And he listed our failings. It was a very familiar list. The trouble with this country, said a man at the back of the hall, is that we are too fond of discussing the trouble with this country. Why don't we talk about our successes?

So we did. Later.

When we gathered in the bar, minus the main speaker, I reminded those remaining of the words of a Frenchman: Britain is the outstanding success story of mankind, he said. I rather spoiled the effect by not being able to remember which Frenchman said that, and when I inquired of a friend present he said he could not remember either, but in any case I had misquoted the man. *England*, the Frenchman said, was the outstanding success story of mankind.

Either way, I said, he was on to something. At a time when half the world appears to be in political turmoil, it does no harm to remind ourselves of the virtues of this country. We cannot take all the credit because being an island has been a huge help, but none the less we have developed a way of going about things which others envy, or should.

It is not that we have a 'national character', if such a thing even exists, but we have certain patterns of collective behaviour, born, I suspect, of the impact upon us of our geography, and our climate. We are a mixed lot – Celts, Romans, Saxons, Danes – who have managed to get along over the centuries. When the Normans came, imagining that they had conquered, they were simply absorbed.

Safe on our island and never for a moment admitting the

123

possibility of defeat, we have developed a confidence in the continuity of our history. Not for us the sudden break, the revolutionary change. We prefer to extend freedom from precedent to precedent.

Because our island has been immune from invasion for nine centuries our institutions have had the chance to develop peacefully – give or take chopping off Charles the First's head. And he was too big for his crown.

We had our moments of turbulence and discontent in the sixteenth and seventeenth centuries but fortunately had almost everything in place before the onset of the problems created by the Industrial Revolution. That is why we coped.

We developed a habit of continuity. Not for us the heady insanity of final solutions. We have a habitual conservatism – a style which informs all political parties alike when they exchange opposition for authority. That is why we allow them to take turns running the country. This presiding spirit of compromise and the comparative insignificance of dogma is the English success story. That is why we are the only sizeable nation in Europe not to lapse into totalitarianism this century.

By this time I was banging on a bit, but the others joined in, warming to the theme. They began to catalogue our national virtues. A language so universal that the world borrows it. A law which is not laid down but built up. A concern not for abstract Liberty but for concrete liberties.

Our forces do not strut, said one. Our politicians do not prate, said another, to something less than universal support. Our ceremony is the best in the world, said a third. By now, the drink was talking.

We are a home-owning, garden-loving, lawn-mowing people, said one chap, overcome.

And the adjectives flew. An inventive people. A talented people. An original people. What us? said a man who had not spoken until then. Yes, we chorused. I tell you what, he said, the real strength of the English is that if they cannot make a success of something, they make a joke of it.

On that cheerful note we adjourned. But I have thought about it a lot since. And it does seem to me that, without boasting or ranting, we should remind ourselves now and then of our successes.

124

It is perhaps relevant that the greatest English man of genius was not a philosopher but a poet. And, as always, Shakespeare put it best:

> This fortress built by Nature for itself
> Against infection and the hand of war . . .

The rest you know, I'm sure.

February 1990

Concerts for Civilisation

Twice in recent years I have introduced a concert by members of the Hallé Orchestra held in the Painted Hall at Chatsworth, the home of the Duke of Devonshire. On both occasions, because these were concerts both by and for the Hallé Orchestra, I have reminded the audiences of this orchestra's beginnings.

In 1857, Manchester staged a great exhibition of the arts in a crystal palace built alongside what is now the central police station. Everyone who was anyone sent works of art to the exhibition, save for the Duke of Devonshire of the day. What, he enquired, do the textile people of Manchester want with art? He soon learned. He visited the exhibition, was greatly impressed, and threw a banquet for the organisers. The greatest attractions of that exhibition, of that festival of arts, were the concerts given in the Free Trade Hall by Mr Hallé and his orchestra.

Charles Hallé, a concert pianist, and a friend of Chopin and Liszt and Berlioz and Mendelssohn and Wagner, had come to Manchester from Paris in 1848 to escape the Revolution. People were too busy killing each other to go to concerts. Hallé was actually German, not French. His name was Carl Halle. But he anglicised his Christian name and added the acute accent to his surname so that people would pronounce it correctly.

In Manchester he gave piano lessons, travelling on the top deck of the horse-drawn trams from pupil to pupil and teaching himself English as he went along. The success of his concerts at the 1857 exhibition persuaded him to launch his own series of Hallé Concerts. The first was on January 30, 1858, and they have been going from that day to this.

126

The purpose of the Chatsworth concerts was to help to ensure that the Hallé concerts continue. When Hallé died in 1895, the good people of Manchester formed a society to run the concerts, and sent for one of the three best conductors in Europe – Hans Richter. He came from Vienna, not on a visit but to live and work in Manchester, and he conducted almost every Hallé concert for the next twelve years. After Richter came Michael Balling, Hamilton Harty, John Barbirolli (for no fewer than twenty-seven years), James Loughran, and now Stanislaw Skrowaczeski.

The Hallé was the first professional orchestra in Britain, the first where the musicians at the performance were the same who had attended the rehearsal – an integrity not always observed elsewhere. For 132 years, the Hallé has demonstrated to the world that Manchester is not simply a city for merchants and manufacturers, but an arena of urban civilisation. Without the Hallé, the life of Manchester would not only be diminished, it would be incomplete.

Music is the greatest of all the arts, both because the form and the content are indistinguishable, and because every live performance, whether of a long-established work or the latest composition, is an act of creation. The concert hall is never a museum, and every concert programme is both a history and a reality. It reminds and it adds. It is a communal experience and a private experience, and people need both. And to ask for money to support music and the arts is not to beg but to enforce. The arts need patronage and they always have. The provision of patronage is the sure sign of civilisation because the arts are the emblem of civilisation.

The subscriber is a patron. Local government is a patron. Government is a patron. But if any of them hesitates and falters, then it is up to us all to take up the responsibility. I went on about this at Chatsworth, arguing that it is important to be conscious of the need to support the arts and to do something about it. We owe it to ourselves, I said, as cultured people. We owe it to those who will come after us. And we owe it to the Hallé – its traditions, its achievements, its performances, and its riches still to come.

Driving home after the second of those concerts, I switched on the car radio and heard the latest news from Europe, from cities known to Hallé and Richter and the rest. It seemed all the more important to make sure that the good things survive and prosper.

March 1990

The Children
of Curiosity

I f Isaac Newton had knocked at your door in 1666 and told
you that the apple which had just fallen from your tree was
governed by the same natural law as the passage of the moon
through the heavens, you could have been forgiven for thinking
that the moon was full and that he was mad.

If the postman had knocked at your door in 1905 and handed
you a copy of the scientific journal containing Albert Einstein's
paper on The Special Theory of Relativity, you could have been
forgiven for taking comfort in what The Times said of his Special
Theory, that it was an affront to commonsense.

It was.

It is very uncommon to recognise at once the value of a piece
of research which is not simply a step forward but a leap into the
unexpected.

I was seized with this thought when I was invited recently to
help to explain and to make known the purpose of a Venture
Research Unit, which is financed by one of the big oil companies
and which is run by a very interesting man.

Today in research laboratories all over the world, scientists
and engineers are trying to answer the question: what next? But
whether the research is described as pure or applied, whether it
is R itself, or only the R in R and D (Research and Development)
its purpose is plain, its intention specific, its outcome possible to
predict. It will only take us one step at a time.

To say that is not to disparage it. Such research is essential to
improvement, to achievement, and to growth. But it can be a bit
narrow, a bit confined, a bit restricting.

And it is getting worse, and not least in this country, where
the fruits of research have to be seen to be of immediate value –

otherwise no money. That is both a government view and an industry view. The code word is relevance; the inspirational phrase – return on investment.

And that is no way to reach the unknown.

But does it matter? As long as relevant research is encouraged and funded is that not the prudent way to progress?

No, it is not.

It may make you better at what you are doing now, but not at what you could be doing in the future. Everything we applaud most now was a discovery not a development. It took us by surprise.

Penicillin is the best example. Polythene is no less apt. And the list is endless. Insulin and DDT. Transistors and lasers. Electron microscopy and holography. The structure of DNA and the development of genetic engineering.

All of them were ready to develop further, but all of them originally were the unexpected product of fundamental inquiry – the children of curiosity.

Scientists came upon the knowledge which made them possible in the course of wide-ranging research. They were not to know when they started what they would discover, but we now all enjoy the benefits of what they discovered. And it will always be thus.

If there is only commissioned research and no creative research the unexpected will never happen. Nor will it if scientists imprison themselves in their own partitioned disciplines. Ideas need freedom.

The new Venture Research Unit has been set up precisely to identify and then to support scientists who are on to something new. But how, I asked, can you choose whom to fund and whom not to fund if the outcome of the research is unpredictable?

The reply was fascinating. The work to be undertaken must be both unique and coherent, not attempted before, of consuming interest but not an obsession.

If it is too general, or too whimsical, or too trivial – if the question asked is little more than: what if? – if it is no more than an excuse to test a new technique – the reply must be: sorry, no.

But if the questions are worth asking, then the answers will be worth having. In what way we cannot know until we know the answers, but what is certain is that new knowledge leads to new science and to new technology.

It is not a matter of being well-informed, it is a matter of knowing more, and that is a very different matter.

The Unit is already backing a few dozen research ventures and is looking for more. It is also following the progress of all the ventures it funds, aware that any transfer from discovery to application will have its difficulties.

Those who claim to know what is best for us can often be wrong. When two men in Manchester built the first computer in the world more than forty years ago, the Government of the day was invited to finance the commercial development.

Its first response was to decline. There will never, it said, be a need in Britain for more than two computers.

And they thought Newton was mad.

April 1990

Take This with a Pinch of Salt

Y ou live in Cheshire, said the man sitting opposite me on the one o'clock train from Euston to Manchester.

Yes I do, I said.

What is Cheshire famous for, he asked, other than a Cat and a Cheese?

Unwittingly he had let himself in for a lecture.

Pass the salt, I said, and I shall tell you.

Cheshire is built on, and has occasionally fallen into, a salt lake, a dead sea, eighty feet deep and two hundred million years old. When the salt water from the sea bubbled to the surface and men found that it was saltier than the water of the ocean they boiled the brine to extract the salt. Where they did that the place came to be called a wich.

So the wiches of Cheshire are not disagreeable old women like the Lancashire witches of Pendle Hill, but towns, salt towns – Northwich, Middlewich, and (no, not Southwich) Nantwich. These three towns were the centre of a thiving salt industry at the time of the Domesday survey and almost certainly flourished in Roman times. Nantwich, whose brine was always weaker than Northwich brine, began to fade as a salt town at the end of the seventeeth century and Winsford took its place.

In the last century the salt field extended east towards Sandbach, but even with that extension, the salt area of Cheshire has never been more than fifteen miles long and seven miles wide, spread across the valley of the Weaver and the Dane and the Wheelock. From there Cheshire supplied, and still supplies, the nation with salt. There are smaller salt fields up and down the country but the Cheshire field is both the biggest and the easiest to tap.

For many centuries salt merchants carried the salt from Cheshire on trains of packhorses along arduous trails long forgotten. But the signposts to those trails linger in local place names – Saltersbrook, Saltersford, Saltergate. For centuries, too, the men in the Cheshire wiches boiled the brine with no thought of where the brine springs came from or why the water was salty. But they discovered the answer in 1670.

The need for more and more fuel to boil the brine and a shortage of wood to burn drove them to prospect for coal. They dug down near Northwich and struck salt, rock salt. There was, as you will have guessed, no coal, because this was a dead sea which had contained no living thing, and therefore no fossils and no fossil fuel. But the salt was rock salt, brown from the sand that had blown over it.

Rock salt required even more fuel than brine to refine it, so they made the River Weaver navigable that it might carry coal into Cheshire and salt out.

The Navigation, as they called it, opened in 1733 and for the next hundred years men made fortunes digging the salt, pumping the brine, emptying the underneath of Cheshire.

And then one day in 1838 a man in Northwich woke to discover that his orchard had fallen 100 feet during the night. Cheshire was caving in. It was paying the price for those centuries of activity when open pan salt works were clustered along the banks of the Weaver by the hundred.

After that they had to go about getting the salt with much greater care, mining it and propping up the roof as they went. There are salt caverns under Cheshire now as big as cathedrals, but the roofs don't fall in.

I thought, said the man opposite, at last getting a word in, that salt was the start of the chemical industry and ICI.

It was, I said. First in Widnes which was handily placed to get the salt from Cheshire plus the limestone and the vitriol and the coal required to manufacture caustic soda. But it was a filthy process and the fumes from the early chemical works poisoned the vegetation for miles and miles around and the sulphurous smell was quite appalling.

Then John Brunner and Ludwig Mond opened a chemical works in the middle of the Cheshire salt field near Northwich to make soda by a better process and swiftly prospered. All the

Widnes firms using the old process united to try to beat off the challenge of Brunner Mond, and eventually they all came together as an amalgamation called Imperial Chemical Industries, ICI.

But they did not invite Roscoe Brunner, who had succeeded John Brunner, to join the Board of the new ICI. Apparently, he had been charging Lever Brothers more than he had charged the CWS (Co-operative Wholesalers Society) for their alkali. Roscoe was very hurt to be spurned in this way and his wife was furious. She spoke out of turn one day, so on November 3, 1926, he shot her and then he shot himself.

By this time my companion on the train was all agog. Tell me more, he said.

Too late, I replied, this is my stop, Macclesfield.

I reached for my bag from the overhead rack. As a matter of interest, I said, who do you work for?

I have just joined ICI, he replied. In marketing.

May 1990

Long May She Reign

O n March 14 this year I received a letter from a friend who is a historian at Oxford. His father was a historian at Cambridge and taught me. Did you know, he wrote, that today Her Majesty the Queen becomes the seventh longest reigning monarch of England, overtaking Ethelred the Unready? I did not know that and instantly informed the nation.

Ethelred came to the throne when he was barely ten. His father Edgar, died in 975, and Ethelred's older brother, Edward, was proclaimed King. Ethelred's supporters were not pleased.

On March 18, 978, Edward came to visit Ethelred at Corfe in Dorset. As he approached the hall where his brother was living Ethelred's retainers came out, gathered round the King's horse as if to greet him, and beat him to death. And the English people learned that violence and treachery had made Ethelred their king.

Ethelred was never allowed to forget it. His brother was commemorated as King Edward the Martyr and his reign was clouded with dissidence and half-suppressed revolt. But I have a soft spot for him because the 'red' in his name comes from the same root as the 'red' in mine and, who knows, we might be related.

But I digress.

My friend's letter did not end with Ethelred. He had much more to tell me. Next year, on February 16, her Majesty will overtake Henry VI. That Henry was looked upon in later centuries as a simple man and a saint. However, the same was not said of his father Henry V, or even less of his grandfather, Henry IV, who had Richard II put to death.

Though it is fair to say that Richard, a temperamental and cultivated man, had been asking for trouble.

But all that will be forgotten in 1996, for in that year, on June 13, Elizabeth II will have reigned longer than Elizabeth I. And as June is the month of the Queen's official birthday, what a celebration that will be.

And there will be more to come. On November 1, 2002. Her Majesty will have reigned for longer than Edward III, who was monarch for fifty years, from 1327 to 1377. He was a warrior by taste and intention, and something of an exhibitionist, which was no bad thing at the time. The Hundred Years War began in his reign.

On February 25, 2008, and I am quoting from my friend's letter, the Queen will overtake Henry III. He reigned for fifty-six years from 1216 to 1272. He was the son of King John and came to the throne at the age of nine, and the barons took unfair advantage of his youth. But he kept his head.

On May 13, 2011, the Queen will overtake George III, who reigned for sixty years, from 1760 to 1820. It is said of him that he saw himself as a latter-day St George at war with the Dragon of Corruption, which is probably true. He was a very serious-minded young man, who, sadly, in old age went slightly off his head. He is said once to have addressed a tree in Windsor Park under the impression that he was speaking to the King of Bavaria.

But he was very much a man of his times.

A new seriousness began to overtake the English in the middle of the eighteenth century. The age of Hogarth and the Rake's Progress gave way to the age of Wesley, and with Wesley the country was in for a religious revival more socially momentous than any in its history.

George was indubitably a good young man, but unfortunately he knew it. He was all too ready to equate his own actions and intentions with the cause of religion and virtue. And if that sounds like a rehearsal for the Victorian age, it was.

Which brings me to the final forecast in my friend's letter.

If Her Majesty is still sovereign on September 11, 2015, she will overtake Queen Victoria and become the longest serving monarch in our history.

Victoria reigned for sixty-four years, from 1837 to 1901. For forty years she was without her beloved Albert. He had guided her through the early years of her reign with his sober sense and his indefatigable energy in the cause of social and domestic righteousness combined with progress in the useful arts and sciences, to quote another teacher of mine.

Albert was the very embodiment of Victorian ideals, and when Victoria withdrew into the role of the Widow at Windsor, there was some public discontent that the nation was not getting value for money from the monarchy.

But first Gladstone and then Disraeli put an end to such chatter. Disraeli, in particular, brought Victoria back into the public gaze and identified her with the destinies of an imperial people. It was his idea to promote her to the title of Empress of India. She had made him the Earl of Beaconsfield in the previous year, and as Punch said: one good turn deserves another.

All this was passing through my mind as I looked at that date in my friend's letter: September 11, 2015.

Is it possible that Her Majesty will still be monarch then?

His next sentence answered that.

If she lives as long as her mother already has, she will be within five days of overtaking her great great grandmother.

The next five days passed in a flash.

The Queen Mother was seen at Cheltenham Races and on the Berlin Wall.

My only fear now is will I be around in 2015 to see it?

God save the Queen.

June 1990

137

Falling for Virginia

Did you know that more Americans were killed in the American Civil War than in the First and Second World Wars combined?

Yes, I did, replied the colleague to whom I had addressed the question. Everybody knows that.

Well I didn't, not until I made a visit to the Shenandoah Valley, a visit which reinforced my view that Virginia is not only the most beautiful State in the United States, but also the most interesting.

Of course, I am prejudiced. I have a granddaughter living in Virginia, and she alone, at two-and-a-half, lights up the place. But with every visit I come away further convinced that Virginia is a place no one should miss. I fell for it on my first visit, when my granddaughter was baptised.

It was Christmas, and in the Old Town of Alexandria, just across the Potomac from Washington DC, where the buildings of this 18th century tobacco port are protected and no one is allowed to build anything out of character, there was a single candle in every window. I took the opportunity then to visit Mount Vernon, the house where George Washington lived, and learned something about the American Revolution.

On my second visit I travelled to the south of the State, to Williamsburg and Jamestown and Yorktown, to learn something about the very first English settlements in America.

This time I went west, heading for the Blue Ridge mountains of Virginia, where Laurel and Hardy went in search of the lonesome pine. I was in search of the Shenandoah National Park and planned to drive the full length of the Skyline Drive which runs for 105 miles along the crest of the Blue Ridge. But the fog beat me to it.

It was so foggy that it was difficult even to find the entrance to the National Park, and when I did the gate was open, there was no one collecting the entrance fee, and there was a sign simply saying: Go right ahead.

That was easier said than done. With visibility down to five yards I crawled in the car until I came to the first exit left and descended into the Shenandoah Valley in defeat.

Two days later, in glorious sunshine, I resumed the Skyline Drive and marvelled at the spectacle all round. But in the meantime I had had two fascinating experiences.

The first was at a new museum at a town called New Market. It is a museum to the Civil War, and it was there that I learned not only about the cruel statistics of that war, but about the bravery too.

Virginia was the principal battlefield. It was there that the war was fought and won. The Shenandoah Valley, which was probably the richest valley in the Southern States, was devastated, with every farm house and every crop destroyed.

Ulysses S. Grant ordered that destruction, and yet when the South surrendered he was magnanimous in victory. And the valley has certainly recovered.

Though I doubt if Thomas Jefferson would have approved either of the Civil War or of its conduct. I was struck by that thought when I went to Monticello, which was Jefferson's home and which is near Charlottesville.

Thomas Jefferson, who wrote the Declaration of Independence, and who to judge from his portrait looked not unlike Voltaire, built Monticello for himself. Monticello is the Italian for little mountain, and Jefferson was the first plantation owner in Virginia to select so elevated a site for his house. Everybody else stayed in the valleys alongside the rivers.

But Jefferson was above all that. And his house, which he designed himself, adding bits and subtracting bits over forty years, is said to reflect the personality of its owner more than any other house in America.

And I am sure that is true. Everything Jefferson gave his mind to, everything he studied, everything he witnessed on his travels,

139

every enthusiasm and every interest is evident in his house. And not only in its contents but in its fitting and structure too.

He collected, he collated, he collaborated. And he always had a reason. He was the pure eighteenth century man, rational and practical.

Where there is a double door in the house, you push one and the other opens too, driven by a chain beneath the floor. The serving door into the dining room revolves. And the huge weight on the calendar clock in the entrance hall goes through a hole in the floor to complete the week.

Everything is both useful and majestic, he did nothing by halves. His house is an accomplishment in every sense.

So too was Jefferson's life.

He served his country as Governor of Virginia, Minister to France, Washington's first Secretary of State, John Adams's Vice President, and finally as President himself from 1801 to 1809.

But he saw these jobs as duties.

He composed his own epitaph which is inscribed on his gravestone.

'Here was buried Thomas Jefferson Author of the Declaration of American Independence of the Statute of Virginia for Religious Freedom and Father of the University of Virginia.'

In other words, and he insisted that there must be not a word more on his gravestone, he wanted to be remembered as a man who believed in political freedom, religious freedom, and intellectual freedom.

So if you are planning a holiday in America, don't just head for Manhattan or L.A., or Florida or the Grand Canyon, go to Virginia for what you can see, what you can learn, and what you can admire.

And go in the Fall.

July/August 1990

At Last,
A Man of Note

I could not bring myself to join in the chorus of dissent which greeted the introduction of the new five pound note this year. Skimpy it may be, discourteous even to Her Majesty, but the Duke of Wellington has been replaced by George Stephenson and his Rocket . . . and not before time. It should have happened 160 years ago.

It was in 1830, on Wednesday September 15, to be precise, that the world's first passenger railway – the Liverpool to Manchester Railway – was opened.

On that great day there were no fewer than eight Rocket-type locomotives including 'Rocket' itself, pulling eight trains. The newest engine was 'Northumbrian', which George Stephenson himself drove. The other seven were driven by his brother, Robert senior, his son Robert junior, four of his assistant engineers, and a little lad called Swanick, a fifteen-year-old apprentice.

Everybody who was anybody was aboard those eight trains – 722 VIPs in thirty gorgeous coaches. And the Duke of Wellington, who was Prime Minister at the time, was the guest of honour. You may wonder why they had not invited the King. George the Fourth had died only three months before, and his successor, William the Fourth, was not considered polite company. His royal absence went unremarked because one event and one event only dominated that great day – the untimely death of William Huskisson, MP, President of the Board of Trade. What happened was this.

Wellington was very unpopular in the North West. He was no longer the hero of Waterloo but the kind of Tory who was thought to be responsible for the Peterloo Massacre, and the authorities were scared to death that the mob would get him. So to ensure his safety, it was decided that his train would have sole use of one of the two tracks from Liverpool to Manchester and the other seven trains would proceed at six-hundred yard intervals on the other line. They were all, of course, travelling in the same direction.

Wellington's train, drawn by 'Northumbrian' and with George Stephenson on the footplate, drew out of Liverpool first to rapturous applause. And because there was no other train on that line Stephenson stopped and started along the way so that the Duke could admire not the scenery but the engineering achievements. 'Magnificent,' he said. 'Stupenduous,' and other noble utterances.

At Parkside, Stephenson stopped to take on water and two trains on the other track, pulled by 'Phoenix' and 'North Star' rattled past. Then a third train arrived, pulled by 'Rocket' and carrying Mr Huskisson. It stopped a little short of Wellington's train. Huskisson and one or two others, in spite of being asked to stay on board, stepped down and walked along the track towards the Duke's train. Wellington leaned out and shook Huskisson's hand. The pair of them had not been on speaking terms so this was a moment of political reconciliation.

It was also the moment at which the man driving 'Rocket' decided to set off again. The passengers on the track either jumped aboard the Duke's train, or took refuge on the embankment. But not poor Huskisson. Overcome by the Duke's cordiality, confused by the noise and stiff from too much kneeling at the late King's funeral, he lost his balance, fell on to the track and 'Rocket' ran over him. 'I have met my death. God forgive me,' he said. In fact, in spite of the panic around him, he did not die there and then. Stephenson uncoupled all but one carriage from 'Northumbrian' and put Huskisson aboard. With two doctors holding a tourniquet to the injured man, Stephenson drove at full speed to Eccles. It was fifteen miles and he averaged thirty-six miles an hour which was actually a world record then but I doubt if anyone recorded it at the time.

The vicar of Eccles took Huskisson in. Stephenson rocketed off to Manchester and brought back three surgeons on the footplate. But to no avail. Huskisson re-wrote his will, signed his name carefully, spoke tenderly to his loved ones, and died at precisely nine o'clock in the evening. As you can imagine, after an incident like that, no one was going to ask: 'Apart from the death of poor Mr Huskisson, how did you enjoy the Grand Opening of the Liverpool to Manchester Railway?' Wellington neither forgave nor forgot. He was against railways, and against Stephenson, until his dying day.

To find out what the first passengers on the first railway journey thought, historians have had to rely on a letter written by the actress, Fanny Kemble. Miss Kemble travelled in Wellington's train on the day of the Grand Opening, but she had had a ride on it three weeks earlier. George Stephenson, with whom, she said, she was 'horribly in love' took her for a trip on the train himself. And it is her letter describing that preview that you will find in every railway history book.

Fanny would have loved the new fiver. But, of course, in her day it would have gone much farther.

September 1990

Port in
a Storm

Every October I take myself away to Blackpool for one party conference or another, and when the proceedings grow tiresome I take the tram up the coast to Fleetwood, to get away from it all.

Fleetwood is not perhaps everyone's choice of a place of escape, but I think it is a town like no other, and I take great pleasure in introducing it to strangers.

Fleetwood was founded 154 years ago by a local landowner, Sir Peter Hesketh-Fleetwood, who named it after himself. It was a product of the railway age. Sir Peter had watched the railway engineers build the main line north from Euston as far as Preston. When they got there the surveyors said they doubted if they could go much further because it would be too difficult to build a line over Shap summit.

Sir Peter saw his chance. With some business friends he set up the Preston and Wyre Railway and Harbour Company, with himself as chairman, and obtained parliamentary permission to construct a railway line from Preston to the land he owned at the mouth of the River Wyre.

There he built a new town, Fleetwood. He invited Decimus Burton, the famous architect who had designed the Doric Arch at Euston station, to plan Fleetwood for him. The pair of them stood on a little mound, which was to become the bandstand of the new municipal park, and decided where the streets should go. It was to be a classical town.

It was also Sir Peter's plan that Fleetwood should be both a port and a resort. The port was to serve not only Ireland and the Isle of Man, but Scotland too, precisely because there was, as yet, no rail link north of Lancaster.

The line to Fleetwood opened 150 years ago, in 1840. Passengers from London got on the train at Euston and got off at Fleetwood. They stayed the night in the North Euston Hotel, which Sir Peter's company owned (and which, incidentally, is still there). The next morning they took the steamship Fire King, also owned by Sir Peter, from Fleetwood to Ardrossan, and then on by train again to Glasgow.

'What more can any reasonable man want?' asked The Railway Times. What a reasonable man wanted was a train all the way from London to Glasgow, and within only a matter of weeks the railway surveyors announced that they could, after all, build a line over Shap.

When that line opened the Fleetwood-Ardrossan trade collapsed.

The railways, too, both provided and then took away Fleetwood's holiday trade. Only six years after the opening of the Preston and Wyre line, branch lines were opened to Blackpool and to Lytham, both of which were already popular holiday centres, and Fleetwood's future as a seaside resort was in doubt.

The classical town which Decimus Burton had planned for Sir Peter was never completed, and that was a great shame because it meant that Fleetwood never attracted either a dormitory commuting population or a retired population.

And Sir Peter's port floundered too. No sooner had it lost its passengers for Scotland to the main line, than it lost its passengers for Belfast to Heysham, and its passengers for the Isle of Man to Liverpool.

Ambitious schemes for the Fleetwod Docks Company (chairman, Sir Peter Hesketh-Fleetwood) were thwarted first by the opening of the Albert Edward Dock in Preston, and then by the opening of the Manchester Ship Canal, which turned Manchester into an international port. The poor port of Fleetwood seemed no sooner to build up a trade than someone else stole it. It was a sad story. A new town that never quite was. A resort which never attracted enough holidaymakers. A port that was filled and emptied again.

But the sea came to its rescue, or rather the harvest of the sea. It became a great fishing port. Twenty-five years ago half of the men in Fleetwood were employed directly or indirectly in the fishing industry, catching fish, or handling fish, or transporting

145

fish. No other town in the North West of England, not even a mill town, was so dependent on one industry. No wonder Fleetwood invented the Fisherman's Friend.

But the fishing industry too has declined, so this October I shall be calling in at the North Euston Hotel to find out what the locals think of the latest plan for Fleetwood. Following a campaign by Lancashire County Council, the Department of Energy has agreed to fund two thirds of the cost of a feasibility study for a tidal energy barrage across the Wyre estuary. It would be both an energy barrage, producing energy without pollution, and a road crossing. It would probably be built upstream of the entrance to Fleetwood Docks and south of the town's disused power station.

Old Sir Peter Hesketh-Fleetwood would, I am sure, have approved of such a development. And so, too, would George Stephenson. He wanted to build a barrage across Morecambe Bay and to run a train across it.

Perhaps we shall be able to cross the Wyre barrage by tram.

October 1990

All Pals Together

'**R**emembrance Day is not what it was,' said the old man with the medals. 'Perhaps we have forgotten.'

He was sitting in a pub in a Lancashire mill town, recovering from the service at the War Memorial. And he reminded those with him of the time when Remembrance Day, Poppy Day, was always November 11, no matter what day of the week.

'The two minutes' silence on a weekday,' he said, 'brought the world to a stop. Now that it is always the second Sunday in November, it is not the same.'

'I take it,' I said, 'that you were in the trenches.'

'I was at the Battle of the Somme,' he replied, and I understood at once why he felt so strongly. Men throughout the kingdom responded eagerly to Kitchener's call to arms in the First World War, but there were more from the North West than from any other region.

Some were inspired by patriotism. Some by a thirst for adventure. Some hoped to escape the mill or the mine or the factory. Some simply wanted a job. But most enlisted because everybody else did.

They lied about their ages, if they were too young, or too old. At Warrington a man of sixty-eight, Henry Webber, a stockbroker, enlisted in the South Lancashire Regiment, and became a subaltern.

They joined up in droves. All the men of a family, of a street, of a community. And the authorities realised there were virtues in keeping friends and acquaintances together, not just in one regiment but in one battalion. All friends together. Pals.

Accrington raised a battalion of a thousand men in ten days, the Accrington Pals, the 11th East Lancs. The 3rd Manchester

Pals was a battalion of Manchester cotton clerks and warehouse-men. Lanchashire as a whole raised fifty-six battalions. Manchester alone raised fifteen. No other city in the country equalled that.

The North West of England responded so enthusiastically to Kitchener's call that it provided the biggest regional contingent of men in the new British army.

And these new recruits found themselves in old and famous regiments. The oldest was the King's Own Royal Regiment at Lancaster. It was the first royal regiment to switch allegiance from James II to William of Orange. After Napoleon escaped from Elba in 1815 the King's Own was sent to Belgium, walked forty-eight miles in thirty hours, and went straight into action at Waterloo.

At Blackburn there was the East Lancashire Regiment, which in a moment of geographical confusion had actually been named the West Lancashire Regiment in 1881, until someone looked at the map and it was hastily renamed. It too had fought with distinction at Waterloo.

At Bury there were the famous Lancashire Fusiliers. They were at the Battle of the Boyne in 1690, and at Culloden. When they fought alongside Frederick the Great of Prussia against the French at Minden in 1758, a French Commander said: 'I have seen what I never thought to be possible, a single line of infantry break through three lines of cavalry, and tumble them to ruins.'

In Manchester in 1914, in addition to the Manchester Regiment, there were two regiments of Hussars. The 14th King's Hussars was known as the Emperor's chambermaids, because they had captured the silver chamber-pot of King Joseph Bonaparte of Spain. The 20th Hussars were known as Nobody's Own. In Warrington, which in those days was in Lancashire not Cheshire, there was the South Lancashire Regiment, one of whose officers in 1914 was Captain C. R. Attlee, later to be Prime Minister. There were three regiments in Cheshire including the 5th Dragoon Guards. Baden Powell had been one of their officers, and so too had Captain Oates, the man who walked out of Scott's tent in the Antarctic saying, 'I am just going outside and may be some time.'

There were thirteen regiments in all in the North West and battalions of all of them went into battle on July 1, 1916, for the

Battle of the Somme. It was the blackest day in the history of the British Army. On that one day Lancashire alone had six thousand men to mourn. Seven hundred Accrington Pals went into action, 585 were killed.

Lord Lonsdale had raised a battalion of the Border Regiment and on that first day of the Battle of the Somme the 11th Lonsdale battalion was in the first line over the top. Twenty-five officers and eight hundred men went into action. Within minutes, twenty-two officers and five hundred men were dead. In all, twenty-seven battalions of men of the North West regiments fought in the Somme on July 1, 1916, and very few survived. When the battle was finally over the casualty toll of the dead and the wounded, on both sides, was over one million.

It is a chilling statistic. I mention it only lest we forget.

November/December 1990

A Link in
the Chain

There is not much merriment in motoring nowadays, but there is one joy unconfined. And that is the moment when you drive into a town you have never been before and the road sign which greets you tells you that the town is twinned with a foreign place you have never heard of before. Where, you ask yourself, is Graft De Rijp, or Braunfels, or Joinville? And what have they in common with Chalfont-St-Giles, or Newbury, or Buckingham?

Sometimes no one lets on. I did not know that Macclesfield is twinned with Eckernforde in Germany and with Hassleholm in Sweden. Nor did I know that Bollington, down the road, is twinned with Thurles in the Republic of Ireland, though I might have guessed. But I would never have imagined that Chester is twinned with Lakewood in Colorado. Is it like Lake Wobegon, I wonder?

Some towns are not only twinnd but quinned. Windsor and Maidenhead, twins in themselves, have 'ring' links, as they call them, with Bad Godesberg, Goslar, St Cloud, Neuilly-sur-Seine, and Frascati. And 'ring' linked towns, I am told, often arrange annual meetings of all the partners. Why? What is the purpose of twinning? And what does it mean?

It has become a common term to describe a special relationship between two communities. In Germany it is called 'partner-schaft', partnership. In the United States they talk of 'sister cities'. And in France they use the word 'jumelage' which suggests almost a blood relationship.

There have always been links between places with a common interest or a particular connection, but since the Second World War people have sought consciously to build up contact and friendship with communities in other countries. It began as part

150

With friendly train in India

Party Conference time !
(Blackpool Gazette and Herald)

On location!

When in China ...

With presentation to Peter Hobday on the thirtieth anniversary of *Today*

With then Archbishop of Canterbury, the Most Reverend Robert Runcie

Shortly after having brought the government down, Thursday 8 March1990

With Cleo Laine and David Hatch,
then Managing Director of BBC Radio

Getting his degree at Durham

Who are you ?
(Denis Thorpe)

At home *(Denis Thorpe)*

With wife, Jenni *(Denis Thorpe)*

With Jenny Agutter
(PIC Photos)

With Lilah *(Denis Thorpe)*

of the peace process, to dispel old enmities, and grew. And it is much more than simply a formal link between two local authorities, and the occasional free trip for local councillors.

Done properly it creates a special relationship between people as well as places. The local authorities can set it up, but it must then involve people of all ages, levels, and interests.

Sometimes the initiative to set up a twinning association comes from a local school or group or organisation and then the local authority is invited to give it its blessing. It certainly works best when as many people as possible take part.

In some towns it is not uncommon for as many as 250 organisations to be involved, ranging from schools and colleges to sports clubs and work groups. In the ones that are really successful there will be exchange visits of every mannor of group from primary school children to handicapped old people. The opportunities it offers are endless.

School groups go in the holidays simply to get to know the other place, and then in term time to study the language as part of the curriculum. Their teachers go to discuss matters of mutual interest with teachers in the twinned town. Sports groups go to compete. Theatre groups go to perform. Church groups go to worship. The deserving go on long-deserved holidays.

People go on business, too. There is a two-way trade in shopping weeks and trade fairs with mutual commercial benefits. It is a fair exchange. And I suspect that we are going to see more and more of it.

In the last few months Bath has been twinned with Kaposvar in Hungary, and Salford with District 11 of Budapest. They will not be alone in seeking links with Eastern Europe. Some towns are looking further afield. Anglesey is now linked with Mafeteng District in Lesotho, Middlesbrough with Masingo in Zimbabwe, and Whitby with Waimea in Hawaii. Captain Cook would have approved of that.

But the great expansion, I am sure, is going to be in Western Europe with the coming of the Single Market. Someone has even composed the text of a Twinning Oath. It goes like this:

> *We,*
> *Being the freely elected representatives of our fellow citizens,*

151

Certain that we interpret the sincere wishes of our populations,

Aware that Western civilisation found its origin in our ancient local communities, and that the spirit of liberty was first recorded in the freedom won by them,

Considering that history must continue in a wider world, but that this world will be truly humane only insofar as men live freely in free cities,

Do take, on this day, a solemn oath to maintain permanent bonds between our two municipalities, to promote exchanges of all kinds between their inhabitants with the aim of fostering, through greater mutual understanding the true spirit of European brotherhood, to combine our efforts in order to further, to the greatest extent within our power, the success of that essential understanding for peace and prosperity: European Unity.

It is quite a mouthful. But it does add meaning to those twinning road signs.

January 1991

152

Northern Echoes

On the very day on which Mrs Thatcher resigned as Prime Minister, and every newspaper talked of 'the end of an era', I received a call from the editor of a national newspaper inviting me to meet his new Northern editor. I accepted at once and said I would be delighted to meet his new colleague in Manchester the following Friday. 'Oh, he's not in Manchester, he works here in London Docklands,' came the reply. 'It is the end of an era,' I said, and I meant it.

For ninety years Manchester was the other end of Fleet Street. Now Fleet Street has gone downstream, and Manchester as a newspaper centre downhill. It is very sad.

On February 3, 1900, in Corton Tank School in Manchester, which had been attended by the children of workers at the nearby LNER engine works, the first Northern editions of the *Daily Mail* were printed. The *Daily Mail* was Britin's first popular national newspaper. It had begun in 1896 and its sale rapidly rose to half a million copies a day. To reach a million its owner, Alfred Harmsworth (later Lord Northcliffe), decided to print in the North as well as in London. He might have chosen Leeds or Sheffield as his second centre, but he chose Manchester and that school in Corton.

His enterprise was immediately rewarded with a daily circulation of a million, and within two years, on November 24, 1902, the *Daily Mail* moved to new premises in Deansgate in Manchester. It was printed there until last year. For on November 3, 1990, printing was transferred to Stoke and Sunderland, the better to facilitate distribution. The new technology has diminished the old presence. Because where Northcliffe had begun, others had followed. The *Daily Express* came to Manchester in

1927 and set up shop in Great Ancoats Street. The *Daily News* came a year later and settled in Derby Street in Cheetham. Two years after it changed its name to the *News Chronicle*.

The *Daily Herald*, the newspaper of the workers, arrived on Oxford Road, Manchester, in 1930, after an enormous rally in Belle Vue. By then Manchester could justly claim to be the other end of Fleet Street. And, of course, it had its own *Manchester Guardian*, whose influence far exceeded its circulation.

But Manchester also had a home-grown newspaper enterprise. As early as 1876 a printer's apprentice called Ned Hulton built a newspaper empire in the city on the twin pillars of the *Sporting Chronicle* and the *Athletic News*. Hulton's premises in Withy Grove in Manchester became the world's largest newspaper printing house.

In 1900, the same year that Northcliffe brought the *Daily Mail* to Manchester, Hulton started the *Daily Dispatch*, which he called the North's own national newspaper. He went on to print other people's morning newspapers, and no fewer than four Sunday newspapers, plus one of the two evening papers in Manchester.

But then the papers began to close. First the *Daily Dispatch*, then the *Sunday Chronicle*, the *Sunday Graphic*, the *Empire News* and the *Sunday Dispatch*. Today no newspapers are printed in Withy Grove, and the building was recently used as the location for a television drama.

There are those who would call this progress. And it is true that the newspaper industry was very slow to adopt the new technology. Bill Pepper, who died last year in his eighties, and who was a newspaper journalist in Manchester for fifty years, said on the day of his retirement: 'It is a sobering thought that we produced today's paper in precisely the same way as we did on the day I joined the paper.'

Not now. The days when a newspaper began from scratch in every printing centre have gone. Now a newspaper can be created in one place and printed in countless places. It is swift, clever, efficient, profitable. But something is missing. And that something is the knowledge that can only come from being present, and away from the capital.

Those at the centre become too inward looking. The northern offices of national newspapers were not extensions but rather

154

alternatives. They saw the world through different eyes. 'London,' you would hear a northern night editor say, 'thinks this is important, but we know it is not, so we shall lead on another story.'

There might be ructions afterwards but a good Northern editor knew when to ignore his masters in London, and he also knew it would delight his staff. This was not narkiness, nor concealed envy. Quite the opposite. Many a Northern editor would argue that people in the North, always provided that they were in gainful employment, could lead a much richer life than those in the South.

And that applied to the newspapers. In the North, the northern editions were expected to be better than those in the South – better written, better informed, better edited. They were closer to their readers and therefore more likely both to learn from their discontent and to profit from their praise. They were encouraged to take the work seriously but not themselves.

All this is not lost. There are teams of excellent journalists in the northern offices of the national newspapers now, but the danger is that they are contributing to their papers not controlling them.

And a Northern editor in an office in London next door to the Editor is there to assist not to resist. In the old days Northern editors may not have been monarchs of all they surveyed, but they were viceroys.

February 1991

Mind over
Matter

Michael Oakeshott, the thinker I admired most in Britain, died at the turn of the year. He was in his early eighties and had published his first book in his early twenties. It was from him that I first came upon a coherent explanation of what I knew to be true – namely that ideas are not pennies from heaven.

Let me explain.

Every human activity, from blowing your nose to running the country, involves knowledge. And universally, Oakeshott argued, this knowledge is of two sorts, both of which are always involved in the concrete activity. He was not, I think, making too much of it to call them two sorts of knowledge, because, although they do not and cannot, in fact, exist separately, there are crucial differences between them.

The first sort of knowledge is technical knowledge, and its principal characteristic is that it can be written down. In other words it is capable of precise formulation.

The second sort of knowledge is practical knowledge. It exists only in practice. It cannot be formulated. It cannot be acquired by learning the rules. It can be acquired only by doing it.

Technical knowledge can be both taught and learned in the simplest meanings of those two words. Practical knowledge can neither be taught nor learned. It can only be imparted and acquired.

It is not enough to follow the rules to indulge in an activity successfully. You have to know how to apply the rules, and far more importantly, you have to know how to go about things. Rules are not sudden insights, gifts from heaven, natural laws, or ultimate principles. They are the abridgement of somebody else's earlier experience of the whole activity. And to engage fully in that activity you have to have the practical knowledge they had when they abstracted the rules.

In other words, until we go about something we cannot know how to go about it. A simple example, which may serve to make this clear, is the activity of cooking.

A cook is not a woman who has a vision of a pie and then tries to make it. A cook is someone practised in cookery and both her projects and her achievements spring from that skill. The rules and principles she follows, the recipes in her cookery book, are the abridgements of the knowledge of others of the activity of cooking. They are a guide to her when she begins her study of cookery but she has to learn by experience not only how to apply those rules but how to go about cooking generally. Only in that way does she acquire the ability to cook, as every mother knows.

Oakeshott believed that it was the great intellectual error of our times to assert that there is no knowledge that is not technical knowledge and to dismiss practical knowledge as a sort of messy ignorance. People, he said, were looking for certainty and missing the point.

The apparent certainty of technical knowledge is itself deceptive. The learning of a technique does not involve starting in pure ignorance and ending in certain knowledge. Nothing, not even the most self-contained technique – the rules of a game – can be imparted to an empty mind, if such a mind can be imagined. What is imparted is nourished by what is already there, the experience.

Oakeshott dismissed the idea of the mind as some kind of bucket waiting to be filled with ideas, or even as some kind of instrument for thinking, a working aparatus, a combine harvester. Mind, he said, is the child of knowledge and activity. It is composed entirely of thoughts. If there are no thoughts, there is no mind. It is not an instrument but a faculty.

Knowledge does not precede conduct, it is a reflection of conduct, the creature of a subsequent analysis of conduct. We can know nothing in advance of activity. Only by indulging in an activity can we learn not only how to overcome difficulties but what difficulties there are to overcome.

And that is why ideologies and ideologists are best avoided. They can only do damage. Oakeshott argued that the politician is never given a fresh start or a clean sheet. He cannot draw up a new plan for a State, or a code of rules which will solve all future problems. Life is not like that, as the people of Eastern Europe will testify.

At any time, however revolutionary a community feels, the arrangements which are enjoyed far exceed those which are seen to be in need of immediate reform. And reform is more often amendment than innovation.

A few hotheads may persuade themselves that there must be a completely new order, but most people regard the greater part of the communal arrangements they have as an inheritance to be enjoyed. And whatever their complaints or dissatisfaction, the amount of their inheritance which they seek to reject is far less than that which they joyfully accept.

Political institutions are not just so many bits of furniture to be moved around at will, they are traditions of behaviour. Separate them from their political and historic context and they don't function, as attempts to export the British Parliamentary system have demonstrated. The truth is that politics is not about problems to be solved, but about difficulties to be overcome. And as one set of difficulties is overcome so another set arises.

There are no ends, no goals, no final whistles. To keep things going with as little damage as possible is what matters. Motive is no excuse. It is not why you did something but the consequence of what you have done by which you will be judged in politics. A point which rarely escapes the electorate.

March 1991

Only Fooling

The son of a friend of mine is getting married on Easter Monday, April 1. When the date was announced an aunt questioned the propriety of choosing April Fool's Day. There is no cause for alarm, said his father, the ceremony will be in the afternoon. Clearly he was brought up in that part of the North of England where, if anyone seeks to make a fool of you after lunch on April Fool's Day, you are entitled to reply:

'Twelve o'clock is past and gone. And you're a fool for making me one.'

In Hampshire, or so I am told, it was the tradition to be even more dismissive:

'April Fool's gone past.
You're the biggest fool at last:
When April Fool comes again
You'll be the biggest fool then.'

Confining the tomfoolery to the morning appears to have been universal. Indeed the ancient book of Calendar Customs is very explicit in its entry for what it calls All Fools Day. 'The custom celebrated on this day,' it says, 'observance of which has not been wholly abandoned, is of an amusing and good-tempered kind, but it is necessary for the one practising it to have regard for the 12 o'clock rule which limited the period of celebration to the morning of the 1st of April.' It then goes on to list some of the means employed in celebrating the custom, a list which I recall first seeing chalked on the blackboard in 1940 in that first magical year of evacuation to a village school.

We townees knew all the obvious japes – the loose shoe lace, the something out of your pocket, the envelope enclosing the blank sheet, the note for delivery to the wrong address, the nonexistent bus terminus. And our mothers had often fooled us with the empty egg-shell inverted in an egg-cup. But we had never offered the innocent pigeon's milk or memory powder, and even less had we heard of two books – the Life of Eve's Mother or the second edition of Cock Robin. I sat the eleven plus in 1940 and mentioned those two books in one of my answers.

No one, however, seems wholly sure when or why the custom and practice of April-fooling began. You will not find it in the second edition of Cock Robin, but in Poor Robin's Almanack, which was published in 1760, there is this observation in verse:

> The first of April, some do say,
> Is set apart for All Fool's Day.
> But why the people call it so,
> Nor I nor they themselves do know.

And that seems to be as true today as it was then.

The first written record in this country of an April Fool is said to be found in Dawks's Newsletter for April 2, 1698, which says that, 'yesterday several persons were sent to the Tower of London to see the annual ceremony of washing the lions in the moat'.

But most historians believe the custom is much older than that. And the commonest explanation both of its antiquity and of its timing is that it was the method of concluding the New Year celebrations.

New Year's Day in Anglo-Saxon England was March 25. Celebrations in those times usually lasted for eight days and therefore April 1 would be the last day of the New Year festivities and a day of great hilarity. There are even those who say that this was a Celtic custom taken up by the English.

The weakness of that explanation is that it overlooks similar ceremonies in France, Sweden, Portgual, and even India. In the second century it was said to be a ceremony to propitiate Risus, the god of Laughter.

In India similar tricks are played at the Holi Festival, which is March 31. So two other explanations can be abandoned. One, that it refers to the uncertainty of the weather at that time of year, and two, that it is a silly mockery of the trial of the Redeemer. Perhaps we owe it all to the Romans. There are those who argue that it is a relic of the Roman Cerealia, which was always held at the beginning of April. The tale is that Proserpina was sporting herself in the Elysian meadows, and had just filled her lap with daffodils, when Pluto carried her off to the lower world. Her mother, Ceres, heard the echo of her screams and went in search of the voice. But her search was a fool's errand. It was hunting the gowk, or looking for the echo of a scream.

In Northumberland an April Fool is a gowk and if you mistime your jape there you hear the reply:

> 'April Gowk Day's past and gone.
> You're a fool and I am none.'

In Yorkshire an April fool is a noddy, but the reply is the same: 'April noddy's past and gone . . . etc.'

But whether it is called April Fool's Day, or April Noddy Day, or April Gowkie Day – in Scotland they use the term gowk (which is properly a cuckoo) for any fool as well as an April fool – the custom lingers on.

It is still the day on which practical jokes of one kind or another are both permitted and expected. At the simplest level children tell one another that their shoe-laces are undone, then shout 'April fool' when the victims glance at their feet.

Now the media have taken it up and are given to including one spurious news item in their deliberation on that day.

It is harmless.

But perhaps Mark Twain got it in perspective in his Pudd'n-head Wilson's Calendar. 'April 1. This is the day upon which we are reminded of what we are on the other three hundred and sixty four.'

April 1991

161

Postal Order

The most famous documentary film made before the Second World War in Britain was Night Mail. Do you remember the wonderful words by the poet W. H. Auden?

> This is the Night Mail
> Crossing the border
> Bringing the cheque
> And the postal order.
> Letters for the rich
> Letters for the poor
> The shop at the corner
> The girl next door . . .

They don't write jingles like that nowadays.

However, a few months ago I was invited to write a sequel to Night Mail, and although I did not presume to imitate Auden I became no less enthusiastic about the subject. I discovered that every day more than fifty million letters are posted in Britain. That is almost one each. Of course some people send more than their share and some people get more than their share, but no matter how many letters are sent from any one place, or how many are delivered to any one place, every letter has to make an individual journey from pillar box to letter box. And that is a delivery task without equal.

Ten years ago everybody said that the days of the letter post were numbered. With the phone and the fax and the character user interface, the letter post would be a dead letter by the end of the century. But they were wrong.

More letters are posted in Britain now than ever before in our history. A hundred and twenty million on the busiest days of the year, 30 per cent up in the last five years alone.

Four out of five are business mail, and half of those are on money matters. Not all are welcome. Some demand, some entreat, some irritate. But countless more matter very much and the nation would be at a loss without them.

The Royal Mail accomplishes something no one else can – the collection from a hundred thousand post boxes and the delivery to twenty-four million addresses of twenty billion letters a year.

The letter post in Britain is the biggest and the best in Europe. It is the only one to make a profit year after year, and the only one where the prices, in real terms, have fallen in the past few years. Even in Germany they charge half as much again to post a letter, and still make a loss. And in most European countries you have to go in search of your mail: it does not come to your front door.

Most letters are posted after four o'clock in the afternoon. First class mail, deemed to be the more urgent and priced accordingly, is handled first – during the evening and the night. Second class mail, deemed to be less urgent, waits its turn and is handled during the daytime hours of the following day.

First class mail is, or should be, delivered the day after it has been posted – and 90 per cent is. Second class mail is, or should be, delivered on the second or third day after it has been posted – and 96 per cent is.

No one in the business pretends that it will ever achieve 100 per cent – life is not like that. Bad weather, transport failures, hold-ups of one kind or another, make that an impossibility. But it can get close. And letters take twice as long in most other countries.

All the mail used to be sorted by hand. It was a laborious process, no matter how deft the operators. Now much of it is mechanised, and concentrated in eight automated offices in the UK.

A machine can sort sixteen thousand letters an hour, and the latest one with an electronic eye, twice that many. And because it is in a hurry it has no time for long-winded addresses. It requires only the postcode, preferably on a separate line.

The British postcode is not a simple number like the American zip code which directs the mail only to the nearest post office, it is a precise definition of an address – the street, the close, the letter box even. But, of course, someone has to take the letter there. The Royal Mail has twenty-eight thousand road vehicles, and they travel three hundred million miles every year. But more than half the mail still travels by rail, on four thousand trains every day.

Nationally, any first class letters posted late in the day for delivery to a distant destination the following morning are sent by travelling post offices – TPOs – special railway carriages fitted out as sorting offices and attached to, or forming, overnight trains. This is the new version of Night Mail.

What, I wonder, would Auden have made of inland post by air, what flight of the imagination? Every night now four million first class letters are carried by air to speed the inland mail. The twin centres of this air network are Speke Airport at Liverpool, and East Midlands Airport near Derby. And a million letters a night are carried by charter flight from London to Edinburgh, and London to Belfast.

But there is one way in which the Royal Mail has never changed since the days of the Penny Black. It still subscribes to the crowning principle that whether a letter travels a few hundred yards from EC1 to EC2, or a few hundred miles from Southend to Sutherland, the price of the postage is the same. It will have no truck with the idea of a mileage rate – a charge for how far.

When Auden finished work on 'Night Mail' he said that a documentary film is a film that tells the truth. But he questioned whether any film could give an exact picture of human life within an organisation. He had a point. It is too easy in the recitation of statistics – of letters posted, miles covered, journeys completed – to overlook the contribution of the people involved. No matter how much automation, computerisation, transportation is introduced, no matter how many man-hours are saved or time more profitably spent, the letter post relies on the efficient use of people. And all its endeavours finally lead to one person taking that last step to your letter box.

Which is why, when I wrote the film, I could not resist as a last line: The British postman has it off pat.

May 1991

It's Nothing to Get Steamed Up About

I t is almost a year since I wrote in this column that I welcomed the replacement of the Duke of Wellington on the new five-pound note by George Stephenson and his Rocket, and I am still getting letters about it – not defending the Duke, but denouncing my statement that the Liverpool-Manchester Railway was the world's first passenger railway.

Rubbish, wrote countless correspondents, the Stockton-Darlington Railway was the world's first public railway. And indeed it was. The Stockton-Darlington opened in 1825; the Liverpool-Manchester five years later.

But . . . in its early years the trains drawn by steam locomotives on the Stockton-Darlington line carried goods only. Horses were used to draw the passenger coaches. It was not until 1833 that steam locomotives were used on the Stockton-Darlington line to draw passenger coaches, by which time the Liverpool-Manchester steam locomotive passenger line was in full service. And although it had opened only five years after the Darlington Line, its locomotives were four times faster than the engines which ran on the North East line.

So, to repeat: Stockton-Darlington was the world's first public railway; Liverpool-Manchester was the world's first passenger railway. End of argument.

Some hope. The passion of railway enthusiasts is like the clamour of steam locomotives. It is also a delight.

Many of the people who wrote to me wanted to know more about the letter which Fanny Kemble, the actress, wrote after being taken for a trip on a train by George Stephenson himself. 'Mr Stephenson,' she wrote, 'explained to me the whole construction of the steam engine, and said he could soon make a famous engineer of me, which, considering the wonderful things he has achieved, I dare not say is impossible.'

She then went on to describe the ride. 'The engine having received its supply of water, the carriage was placed behind it, for it cannot turn, and was set off at its utmost speed, 35 miles an hour, swifter than a bird flies (for they tried the experiment with a snipe). You cannot conceive what the sensation of cutting the air was; the motion is as smooth as possible, too. I could either have read or written; and as it was I stood up, and with my bonnet off "drank the air before me". The wind, which was strong, or perhaps the force of our own thrusting against it absolutely weighed my eyelids down. When I closed my eyes this sensation of flying was quite delightful, and strange beyond description; yet strange as it was, I had a perfect sense of security, and not the slightest fear.'

Not everyone who travelled on those first trains had no fear. Twelve years ago, in a television programme about the opening of the Liverpool-Manchester Railway, a history master in the North West made public a letter written by one of his ancestors in 1835. It described his first trip on a train from Manchester to Liverpool. 'A few minutes after seven we started, not very fast at first, but in less than five minutes, off we went like a shot from a gun. No sooner did we come to a field than it was a mile behind us. But this was nothing in comparison with meeting a long train of carriages from Liverpool.

'I was never so frightened in my life as at this moment. I shrank back completely horrified in my seat. I do not think the train was more than two seconds in passing, yet it was as long as Holywell Hill. We were then going at full thirty-four miles an hour. Consequently they passed us at double that time. It is impossible to form any idea of the rapidity of moving. Several other trains passed us, but as I was aware of their approach, they no longer alarmed me. The first seventeen miles we went in thirty-two minutes.

'I am much disappointed in the view of the country, the railway being cut through so many hills, you have frequently for miles only clay mounds on each side of you. Consequently no splendid prospect can attract your attention.

'Even when the railway is on a bridge, or at an elevation above the usual track of land, you are not charmed by that diversity of prospect to be met with in ordinary stage coach travelling, which has a decided superiority over this new work of man. It was an hour and a quarter going the thirty-three miles, the latter part of the journey being performed at the slow speed of twenty miles an hour. Previous to entering Liverpool you go through a dark, black, ugly, vile, abominable tunnel which has all the horrors of banishment from life, such a hole as I never wish to go through again, unless my time is as precious as it was the other day . . .'

Clearly he found train travel more of an ordeal than a delight. Only the speed redeemed it for him. When George Stephenson built that 'dark, black, ugly, vile, abominable tunnel' only a few years previously, he had it whitewashed and hung with lights so that people could walk through it.

None the less, as a later historian said, 'The Liverpool and Manchester Railway showed the world what could be done and led to the greatest change in the habits of mankind that has ever come about.'

But that cannot be the last word. I have it from the Mayor of Stockton-on-Tees himself that on September 27, 1825, Stephenson's Locomotion No 1 arrived in Stockton having just hauled a train with some six hundred passengers aboard for South Durham, via Darlington, to Stockton. This, he says, was the world's first passenger train.

So perhaps the truth is that Stockton-Darlington had the first passenger train. Liverpool-Manchester the first passenger service.

Discuss.

June 1991

167

Kippers and
Customs

Midsummer Day used to be July 5. On the Isle of Man, it
still is. That is the day of the Tynwald Ceremony, when
the Manx Parliament meets in the open air, on Tynwald Hill at
St John's, near Peel, to proclaim the laws enacted in the previous
year. Sir John Betjemen once said that he had always imagined
the Isle of Man to be a mountain wreathed in mist and
surrounded by a cinder track. Then he went to see it for himself
and was bowled over.

The Isle of Man is an island unto itself. It is not part of
England, in the sense of being an off-shore island. It is an ancient
kingdom, and Tynwald was founded by King Orry in 938 AD.
Celtic missionaries from Ireland visited the island 1,500 years
ago. The Vikings conquered it in about 800 AD and made it the
capital of the Kingdom of the Isles which then included the
Hebrides.

In 1105 the sovereignty of the Isle of Man was granted to
the Stanley family – ancestors of Lord Derby – who ruled it
first as kings and then as lords for more than eight hundred
years.

But in 1765, much disturbed by the 'smuggling mischief', the
British Government passed the Revesting and Mischief Act,
which not only invested sovereignty once more in the Crown,
but also diverted all Customs and Excise duties to the British
Exchequer. A century later, Britain agreed that the Isle of Man
could keep the Customs revenues, provided that Britain dictated
how the money should be spent.

A century later again, in 1958, Britain agreed that the island
could spend the Customs revenue as it chose. Fifteen years ago
the Isle of Man demanded the right to levy whatever Customs

and Excise duties it thought fit. It is not part of 'the realm of England but an estate and domain of the Crown of England'.

Catering for the summer visitor has been the main Manx industry for more than one hundred years. When the Victorian Pier at Douglas was opened in 1873 the number of annual holiday makers was 90,000. More hotels were built, the roads were widened, the narrow gauge railway opened, and in 1913 no fewer than 634,512 visitors arrived on the island, most of them from the North West of England. That figure has never been surpassed.

There was a brief period just after the Second World War when the annual numbers were over 600,000, but since then the number has rarely passed half a million. Not that the islanders have given in. The opening of the casino in 1963, of the first commercial radio station in 1964, of the new sea terminal in 1965, were all signs of enterprise. But the disaster at Summerlands in 1973 was not only a tragedy in itself, it was also a serious setback to the island's tourist reputation.

Indeed, it was a Radio 4 programme earlier this year about the Summerlands disaster which set me thinking again about the Isle of Man. I used to go every year to the TT Races, in the days when I was a motor racing correspondent. I was there that famous year when Geoff Duke clocked up the first hundred-mile-an-hour lap, and then the timekeeper discovered his sums were wrong and it was only 99.97 mph.

I also went every year when I was an industrial correspondent because several trade unions favoured it for their annual conference location. And I have very happy memories of going to the Isle of Man music festival.

It is, of course, a favourite retirement place especially for people from the North West of England, not least because of the tax laws. I once made a radio programme, I recall, called 'A Little Bit of Haven', which was about its tax advantages. But even in that I took care to point out its other virtues. It is a haven, in the strict sense of a place of safety and refuge, meant to be enjoyed.

Anyone who knows the island, who has been up the Snaefell Mountain Railway, who has seen Laxey and Ramsey, Port Erin and Port St Mary, and who has seen the sun set over the Port of Peel, the Sunset City of the West, will tell you that there is nowhere which encompasses quite so much in such a small space. Its days of mass tourism may be a thing of the past, but it is a must for the discriminating visitor. Especially for those who like a kipper for breakfast.

July/August 1991

170

Assateague, Chincoteague

Where did you go for your holidays this year? That, according to an article I read in an airline magazine (and it could be special pleading), is the third most common question asked of one friend by another. The article did not indicate which are the two most common questions, but I imagine that they are:

1. How are you?
2. Where did you leave the car?

The commonest responses to the answer to the third most common question are either:

We went there last year. Or: We must go there sometime.

This year, quite by chance, I confounded all that dialogue. Asked: where did you go for your holidays this year? I replied: Assateague and Chincoteague. Mouths fell open. Where? they asked.

Assateague and Chincoteague, two islands off the coast of Virginia. I have written here before about the virtues of Virginia, a State I visit regularly because my eldest son and my eldest daughter-in-law and my eldest granddaughter live there. And it was their idea this year that we should explore Chesapeake Bay.

So off we set. We went first to Annapolis, the capital city of the State of Maryland, which for a few months in 1784 was the capital of America, the seat of the national government. Annapolis is proud of its history. It describes itself as a museum without velvet ropes or plastic covers and it certainly takes care of its historic buildings.

It has restored the house and the garden of William Paca, who was Governor of Maryland and one of the men who signed the Declaration of Independence. His house was built between 1763 and 1765. Early this century it became a commercial hotel and

171

hostelry and the garden became a concrete car park and the whole place began to look run down.

In 1965 a developer decided to knock the whole thing down to build a towering glass and steel office block. And that, you will agree, is no way to celebrate a bi-centenary. The local historical foundation stepped in and stopped the demolition, and the house and garden have now been restored to their original splendour.

From there we went down the east coast of Chesapeake Bay to Wades Point Inn. Wades Point gets its name from Zachary Wade, who received a grant of the land in 1657. The inn was built around 1819 by Thomas Kemp, one of the famous ship-wrights of Baltimore who built the Baltimore Clippers, the fast sailing ships which helped America to win the war of 1812.

Wades Point is near St Michaels, which is known as the town that fooled the British, because in that war on one August night the British ships shelled the town. But the residents had imposed a blackout, the first in recorded history. They turned out all the lights in their houses and hoisted lanterns into the treetops.

The British gunners aimed high, the plan worked, and only one house was struck. It is now known as Cannonball House.

From there we drove south, through Cambridge and Salis-bury, and we crossed the border from Maryland into Virginia before turning east to the islands. Both Chincoteague and Assateague are nature reserves. Chincoteague (the name comes from an Indian word meaning 'beautiful land across the water') is a National Wildlife Refuge, but it is also Virginia's only resort island.

That is where we lodged. It is a small fishing village on an island seven miles long and a mile-and-a-half wide. It is famous for its flowers: flowers of the field like dog fennel and horse nettle; flowers of the forest like trumpet creeper and rough bedstraw; flowers of the marsh like rose mallow and arrow arum. It is also famous for its birds: loons and grebes, shearwaters and storm petrels, gannet and pelicans and cormorants, bitterns and herons and ibises, swans and geese and ducks, vultures and hawks and falcons, quail and rails and coot, plus many more.

And then there are the Chincoteague ponies, who, strictly speaking, are not wild but feral, descendents of domestic animals who have reverted to a wild state. Assateague, which shelters Chincoteague from the Atlantic, is a barrier island built by sand that persistent waves have raised from the ocean's gently sloping bed. It is constantly reshaped.

It has everything and more that Chincoteague has, except houses and shops and restaurants. You drive across, there is somewhere to park, there is a visitor centre, but the rest is nature, with a beach as long and beautiful as any I have ever seen. I lay on it, walked on it, built sandcastles on it.

This, my three-year-old granddaughter said, is a proper holiday. And she was right.

You must go there sometime.

September 1991

A Grand Day
for the Family

The last Saturday in September was Grandparents' Day. If
you are a grandparent and you are reading this before the
last Saturday in September, lucky you. It means that the October
issue of *Saga* has reached you early, and you can tell your
grandchildren what is expected of them, and from them, on
Grandparents' Day. Like Mothers' Day and Fathers' Day and
for that matter Christmas Day, Grandparents' Day has its
commercial side. It is even sponsored by the makers and sellers
of greetings cards and chocolates and little gifts. But it has a
more serious purpose.

Grandparents' Day was invented last year by Age Concern,
which considers that grandparents are a threatened species. The
Charity argued that we could be excused for thinking that
grandparents have become more or less extinct this century, so
little do we hear about them. It blames social mobility – families
far-flung, and the increase in divorce – families divided. Since
then it has conducted a survey of grandparents which has
revealed that older grandparents have more grandchildren but
see them less fequently. All is not gloom, however. More than
half of all grandparents see their grandchildren at least once a
week. But one in six of grandparents over the age of sixty-five
see their grandchildren less than twice a year.

Nine out of ten of all grandparents give their grandchildren
regular presents. Half of all grandparents give their grandchildren regular advice and have them to stay. But as grandchildren grow older and move away to live independent lives
they grow out of touch with their grandparents. And an increasing number of grandparents who in their youth knew their own
grandparents say that relationship was closer than the one they

have now with their grandchildren. If that is true, says Age Concern, then it is a matter for concern, because grandparents now live longer than in previous generations and could face lonely futures if families lose touch.

Grandparents' Day is a first attempt to avert such unhappiness. Its purpose is to remind us all, young and old alike, that grandparents are very important people precisely because they have been around for a long time. They know what went before and children long to know where they came from and to hear about family history. Grandparents are also useful. They can babysit, advise, listen.

They do not have the same responsibilities as parents. They do not need to exercise as much authority. They can be more easy-going and indulgent. My grandfather, my father's father, was like that. When I was little, he was my best friend. Whenever I was in trouble I rushed to him because he believed I could do no wrong. A view I shared. And in dealing with my grandchildren now, I can see who I take after.

Indeed for me, and I suspect for countless other grandparents, the last Saturday in September is Grandchildren Day, yet another excuse for making a fuss of them. It is not indulgent, even less over-indulgent. It is rather a reminder that family life is our real history, and the emblem of our existence. It is the context of living.

And to be excluded from the enjoyment of that, at either end of your life, however long or short your lifespan, is to be diminished.

There has been much talk lately of restoring family values. But too often it has been selective, an endorsement of chosen patterns of behaviour, of particular achievements and rewards. And life is richer than that. Every family is an old family because we all go back forever, or for at least as far as evolution will allow. We all have ancestors and most of us will be ancestors. If we are grandparents we already are.

That is not something to swank about but it is something to enjoy. There is a lot to be said for having good relations with your relations.

Perhaps, therefore, we should look upon Grandparents' Day as another Christmas, a second Christmas, concerned not simply with the Holy Family but with every family.

October 1991

At Whose Service?

As Honorary Life President of the Friends of the M6, I have never known a year like it. Letters by every post. But not the usual chorus of complaints about cones and contra-flows, and why the longest delays are where the motorway passes the RAC control centre. No, this year the main concern has been a proposal to build the biggest motorway service station in the country practically on my doorstep. Over our dead bodies, say the Friends.

Junction 19 on the M6 is the turn-off for Macclesfield, centre of the universe. The Knutsford service station is a few hundred yards south of Junction 19, and motorists with local knowledge frequently use it as a cunning means of entrance to, or exit from, the M6. But the service station is to be closed to make way for a new road linking the M6 and the M56. In its place, the Department of Transport wants to build a new motorway services area seven times bigger than the Knutsford station.

It would cover fifty acres. It would have parking space for more than one thousand cars and more than three hundred lorries. It would have shops, fast food counters, cafeterias, an amusement arcade, even a motel. It would be illuminated night and day. And it would sit slap bang in the middle of one of the last stretches of unspoiled countryside in North Cheshire.

So much for the green belt.

The Department wants to locate the new services area two miles north of Junction 19 on the M6 and a glance at any map will reveal the folly of that. It is the last piece of rural Cheshire before the M56 which is the southern boundary of the great built-up areas of Greater Manchester and Merseyside. It is a much loved part of the county and is the area surrounding Arley Hall, one of the most popular stately homes in Cheshire.

The locals are livid. They have even set up a defence association, which is housed in the East Wing of Arley Hall. Their opposition to the scheme has been endorsed by the county council and by Macclesfield Borough Council, whose planning committee unanimously rejected the idea. But this is more than a little local difficulty. It would, indeed, be outrageous if this service station were to be built. It is not even needed.

A motorist keeping within the law can drive from the Sandbach services to the Charnock Richard services on the M6 in less than half an hour. But the Department of Transport has got it into its head that motorway service areas should be in the open countryside and not in built-up areas.

Why? Because it is cheaper. And because the Department can make a profit: it can buy land by compulsory purchase in the middle of the country at agricultural prices, and sell it to the motorway service operators at development value.

What, then, became of planning policy? Answer: it is beginning to re-assert itself.

This summer the Minister for Planning at the Department of the Environment said NO WAY (or words to that effect) when the Department of Transport said it wanted to build a hundred-acre motorway services area on the M40 at Tetsworth in Oxfordshire.

Pause for applause.

However, let us not get carried away. The Department of Transport still has some daft ideas. It is said to have considered twelve alternative sites for the M6 service area but it will not let on where. It is being secretive, no doubt, because it still clings to the belief that motorway service areas should be sited in open country.

It should look more carefully at the Minister of Planning's published objections to its Tetsworth proposal. The site is in open countryside, he said, and the need for the service area is outweighed by environmental implications.

Precisely.

Motorway service areas should be treated as commercial developments and should be located close to towns and industrial areas. Then everyone can enjoy the countryside.

November/December 1991

Whither Macclesfield?

I have been taken to task for misplacing Macclesfield. Me of all people.

I have only myself to blame. I committed myself in print to the following statement:

'Macclesfield is not, and never was, in Mercia.'

Nonsense, replied a chorus of critics. You have only to look at an old map to see that Mercia reached as far north as the River Lune.

And indeed, a man I know recently bought a house in Upper Ribblesdale and was cheerfully assured by the estate agent that his new home sits on the border of the ancient kingdoms of Mercia and Northumbria.

So Macclesfield must have been in Mercia.

Yes, but . . .

Mercia had ceased to matter long before Macclesfield had a name, let alone an identity. In other words, Macclesfield was never in Mercia because it was not around at the time.

Let me explain.

When the Venerable Bede was writing his Ecclesiastical History of England, in the early years of the eighth century, he had two great worries about his own times.

He feared that the young men of his own Northumbria were far too fond of entering monasteries not to serve God but to dodge military service and to avoid paying taxes.

He also feared that the kings of Mercia would take advantage of this and seek to repeat the achievements of Penda, who had invaded Northumbria in the previous century and slain its king, Edwin, and then returned to slay the saintly Oswald.

Bede was right to be worried.

In the eighth century Mercia produced two powerful rulers in succession, each of whom ruled for forty years, Ethelbald and Offa.

For almost the whole of his reign, Ethelbald was the undisputed overlord of England from the Humber to the Channel. But he was a tyrant, and one night in 757 he was murdered by a member of his bodyguard.

After a brief spell of civil war, Offa succeeded to the kingdom of Mercia. He was probably the best Anglo-Saxon ruler before Alfred the Great. He built Offa's Dyke, stretching from the Severn to the Dee, to define the boundary between his people and the Welsh.

When Offa died in 796 everyone assumed that Mercia would maintain its commanding position. But less than thirty years later Mercia was overthrown by Egbert of Wessex.

It had another brief spell of independance, and then the Vikings came. In 865 a great army of them landed in East Anglia and in a series of swift campaigns over the next five years, they destroyed the ancient kingdoms of East Anglia and Northumbria, and of Mercia too.

Only Wessex withstood the onslaught. And it fell to the subsequent kings of Wessex, Alfred, Edward, and Athelstan, to create the kingdom of England.

Mercia remained a name on the map but it was no longer a power in the land. Its great days were over.

And where was Macclesfield all this time?

Answer: still to come.

Nobody knows for sure when Macclesfield was founded. Some time before the eleventh century, says its official historian.

Nor does anyone know where it got its name, or how, or when.

What little evidence there is would suggest that it was a small Saxon settlement of the late tenth century, probably in the reign of Ethelred the Unready, who came to the throne in 978.

What is beyond dispute is that when Edward the Confessor came to the throne in 1043, Macclesfield not only existed under its own name, but was worth £8, a sizeable sum for a village settlement in those days.

That prosperity did not last long.

After William the Conqueror's successful invasion in 1066, the North of England rose against him.

His army took its revenge, laying waste the land and slaughtering the inhabitants.

It was a disaster for Macclesfield. The Domesday Book, published in 1086, describes Macclesfield as a settlement worth only £1, with a workforce of only four serfs.

But, having taken with one hand. William gave with the other. He gave the Earldom of Chester to his nephew, Hugh, and with it the village of Macclesfield.

Over the next century the village prospered and the population grew. The villagers gave their allegiance not to some distant memory of Mercia (a name still bandied about) but to the Earl of Chester and Lord of the Manor of Macclesfield.

When the seventh Earl of Chester, John the Scot, died in 1238, leaving only two young daughters, the King, Henry III, took the earldom for the crown.

'We are unwilling so illustrious an inheritance should fall under the divided sway of the distaffs of women,' he said.

The Earl's estates within the county went with the earldom and so the Manor of Macclesfield became crown property.

Henry gave it to his son, Edward. And when he became King Edward I, he granted Macclesfield a Royal Charter.

That was in 1261, and the rest, as they say, is recorded history.

All of which, I hope, goes to explain why I argue that Macclesfield is not, and never was, in Mercia, as the Black Prince, who came to Macclesfield for his holidays in the fourteenth century, clearly understood.

But not everyone agrees.

I got into this argument because I was trying to persuade the National Trust to redraw the boundaries of its regions to put Macclesfield where it belongs – in the North West of England, not in the West Midlands.

The National Trust actually uses the term Mercia Region to define the area which embraces Cheshire, Greater Manchester, Merseyside, Shropshire, Staffordshire, and the northern part of the West Midlands county.

A Wilmslow man wrote to the Trust urging it to stand firm and keep Macclesfield in Mercia. And I, he said, must reconcile myself to the fact that I live in the North Midlands.

That *is* nonsense.

Perhaps I should send him a map and a compass, then he can work out where Cheshire is.

January 1992

The Brains
in Spain

Nineteen-ninety-two, said a man I met in Madrid in 1991, will be our year. Madrid will be the international City of Culture. Barcelona will host the Olympic Games. Seville will be the location of the World Expo. What will you in Britain do? Funny you should ask that, I said. A member of Her Majesty's Government put the same question to me. He was showing me one set of plans for the British Pavilion at the World Expo in Seville, and he invited my comments. I studied the plans carefully and then told him that this was an opportunity for a proclamation of unashamed patriotism.

Explain yourself, he said.

Well, I said, if you were to build this Pavilion as planned, and if I were to be there for the opening day of the Expo, this is what I would want to say to the nation back home.

'Good morning from Seville, where today the King of Spain will open the World Expo '92. Columbus left here five hundred years ago to discover America. When the King of Spain arrives here this morning, he will discover Britain. To step into this British Pavillion is to get to know us, and to marvel at the originality that is Britain. This Pavilion not only says it, it proves it. You can't miss the British Pavilion. It has the best site, and it is the first thing you notice when you get here. From the outside it is like a high-tech think-tank bursting with ideas. Even the hundred foot wide Union flag hovering over the entrance is built-in. From the inside, because you are now in Britain, you can look out through the flag which is translucent.

'Inside and out there are great cascades of water, echoes of oceans and oceanography, which are there not only to remind you that when you are in Britain you are in and on an island, but also – and this is very clever – to demonstrate that Britain is inventive, creative, ingenious. In short, original. It takes you, as it were, from Dogger Bank to Jodrell Bank. They call it the Brainwave. You catch glimpses of all the great brains of Britain, from Newton to now, their ideas spinning forth, wave upon wave, ceaselessly ahead. But I am ahead of myself.

'You have to queue to get in here. And rightly so. Britain invented the orderly queue. But this one is like no other. You are entertained (and educated) at every step, with much wit and wisdom. Clearly we have now invented electronic busking. There are video clips of cartoons and commercials, live transmissions from the Commons and the cricket. It is all in English, but again rightly so. English is now the world's first language, and everybody else's second language.

'So right from the start you get the impression that the British are original, given to invention, to self-perception, accomplished, and funny with it. It is a great introduction. The best queue I have ever been in. Once inside, you do not look about in desperation, wondering what to do and where to go. You are taken by the hand on an adventure, a voyage of discovery.

'A great curved video wall – alive with presentations – lures you in, there to witness a live stage presentation of theatre, comedy, dance, music, fashion. Ten minutes of that and a second curved video wall starts you on your travels. You board the first travellator, and as it carries you up to the first level of the Pavilion, you see the Brainwaves from the other side, whirling beneath you.

'And then as you move towards the first Pod, even the handrail alerts you to what you are there to discover. It offers clues to understanding Britain.

'Pod One is the place and the people. Not the usual tourist images – the Yeomen of the Guard and a clutch of royal palaces – but the then and the now and the always. A demonstration that history is what people make of their geography. This Pod, which revolves, really turns people's heads. In Pod Two, the theatre, everybody sits down, three hundred at a time, for everything from a Pop Festival at Wembley to the Last Night at the Proms; from a first night at the National, to the umpteenth performance of Starlight Express. This is cultural Britain, world leader in music and musicals, in drama and acting, in architecture and design, in broadcast and in print.

'The visitors emerge from Pod Two, the theatre, on to this terrace, free now to reflect upon what they have seen and upon what they now see. The Flash of Inspiration, the outcome of the brainwaves. Among themselves, I believe, the designers of this British Pavilion called this The Great Wheeze, but that does not translate very easily into Spanish.

'But it is a great wheeze, a man-made pulsar, a quasar even. Once you have seen it, you have seen the light. You turn from it and begin to descend, down past a great image wall, a mosaic of high technology, on which all the leading British companies are displaying not only their products but their imagination and originality. You go down to the concourse and to the present, to the world of work, of engineering and design, of technology and achievement – the world of the makers and of the market makers. In the shop you can buy British. Downstairs in the restaurant you can enjoy a Taste of Britain. And this is not the end.

'The signs do not read This Way Out but This Way On. The climax of the voyage of discovery is not to admire what is, but to explore what will be. You gather around the base of the Flash of Inspiration where there are banks of interactive terminals with which you can literally touch upon the truth about Original Britain. You can put your finger on it.' The minister stopped me there. I do not know whether I convinced him; I must go to Seville in the spring and see for myself.

February 1992

Witches and
Wapping Lies

The most famous naked lady in the English speaking world is, I would imagine, Lady Godiva. She, you will recall, rode naked upon a horse through the streets of Coventry in 1040 to demonstrate against her husband's cruelty to his tenants. They, gentlemen almost to a man, looked the other way so as not to embarrass the brave and shivering lady. And her husband was so ashamed that she should have been driven to this desperate length that he changed his ways and was kind ever after.

There was one rude tenant who did not avert his gaze. He was a tailor called Tom; hence Peeping Tom.

To this day, in countless village fêtes up and down England, nubile young women with a touch of exhibitionism recreate Lady Godiva's ride, suitably screened in body stockings and long blonde wigs.

But not in March. It is a little early in the year for such antics. Though it used to be earlier, Lady Day, March 25, was, until 240 years ago, the legal beginning of the New Year. It may not be the appropriate day to remember Lady Godiva, but it is precisely the right day to recall another lady in English history who made an even braver demonstration against her husband's miserliness and tyranny.

Her name is Lady Mabel (or Mabella) Tichborne, and she is remembered every year in her own parish on Lady Day. In the year 1150, she was lying on her death bed and she asked her husband to bequeath land to a charity to provide the income for an annual distribution of bread to the poor. Her cruel and mean-minded husband said that he would bequeath only as much land as she could cross. Obviously he was thinking that because of her age and her illness – she was, after all, bedridden and dying – she would not be able to travel any distance at all.

But she did. With the aid of her maid, she climbed from her bed and crawled on all fours over twenty-three acres of land. It must have been painful for her and for those who watched, but to this day those acres of land are known as 'the crawls'.

And every year, on Lady Day, the inhabitants of the parishes of Tichborne, Cheriton, and Lane End, in Hampshire, receive a measure of flour with which to bake bread. The flour is paid for from the rent of 'the crawls'. The Tichborne Dole, as this bequest is called, is distributed at a public ceremony held in the grounds of Tichborne House. The ceremony begins with the blessing of the flour, and ends with a prayer for the soul of Lady Mabella Tichborne.

I think she deserves it. Although she was something of a witch. Legend has it that when she crawled round the twenty-three acres brandishing a burning torch, she prophesied that if the charity were allowed to lapse, seven sons would be born to the family, followed by seven daughters, and the title would lapse.

She was not far wrong.

The Tichborne Dole was stopped after 644 years. Whereupon the then baronet had seven sons, and his heir had seven daughters. His third son decided that something must be done to ward off the curse of his famous ancestor. So he revived the Dole and changed his name to Doughty.

The title became extinct in 1968 with the death of Sir Anthony Doughty-Tichborne, the fourteenth baronet. But the Dole continues, and so does the fame of the family. It was the subject of the most celebrated case of impersonation in English law.

In March 1853, Roger Charles Tichborne, the heir to the ancient baronetcy, set sail for Valparaiso. He spent a few months wandering around South America, and then, on April 20, 1854, he embarked on a sailing ship named *The Bella*, bound for Jamaica. The ship went down and nothing more was seen or heard of Roger Charles Tichborne . . . until October 1865.

In that month, in Wagga Wagga, in Australia, a man who had been known locally as Tom Castro, announced that he was R. C. Tichborne. On Christmas Day, 1866, he landed in England, insisted that he was the lost Roger and claimed the Tichborne baronetcy. Lady Tichborne, the mother of the real Roger, claimed to recognise him, but the rest of the family would have none of it, and none of him.

The case went to court where the man's claims were proved to be false. He was identified as Arthur Orton, the son of a Wapping butcher. Orton was then tried for perjury, a trial which lasted for 188 days.

He was found guilty and sent to prison for fourteen years.

Punishment for telling such a wapping lie.

March 1992

Give Me the
Moonlight

W eeks before Christmas, I listened to an argument about Easter. The participants were two politicians from the same party arguing about the date of the election. One argued: no later than April; the other: no earlier than May. The former fumed. If we go to the polls on May 7, the campaign will begin on Maundy Thursday, trample on Easter weekend, interrupt the fortnight's school holiday, trip over the May Day holiday Monday, and leave us only two clear days to knock on doors. His colleague groaned. You have a point, he said. It beats me why Easter cannot always be the last weekend in March. It was last year. And Easter Monday was April Fool's Day, I said, interrupting them. A good day for an election. They raised their eyes to heaven. It is no good looking there for inspiration, I said, we've been through all that. All right, clever clogs, said the one with the marginal seat in Lancashire, explain. So I did.

The early Christians, I said, celebrated Easter on the first day of Passover, and that is not necessarily a Sunday. This year it is a Saturday. It was at the Council of Nicea in 325 AD that they settled on a Sunday. They had intended to meet at Ancyra in Galatia until the Emperor Constantine wrote to all the bishops. 'Come to Nicea in Bithynai,' he said, 'it has excellent weather and I myself will be able to take part in and mark your discussions.' Who does that remind you of? said the marginalised one to the other.

It was, I continued, an invitation none dare refuse, and they came up with a formula for calculating the date of Easter. Easter Day, they said, would always be the first Sunday after the full moon which happens upon or next after the 21st of March. And if the full moon happens upon a Sunday, Easter Day will be the following Sunday. And it follows from this that Easter Sunday can never be earlier than March 22 and never later than April 25. This year it is April 19, last year it was March 31.

But I thought, said the one with the safer seat, that they argued about this for years. Bede says so. Yes, I said, for three centuries the Celtic Church ignored this calculation and had its own date for Easter, until Oswy, the King of Northumbria, who followed the Celtic way, had an argument over breakfast with his wife, who followed the Roman way, about when to eat eggs during Lent.

To settle the matter he summoned a Synod at Whitby in 664 AD. They argued about the lunar cycle and the solar cycle for hour after hour until the King had had enough. 'On whose authority do you, Coleman, speak?' he asked. 'St Columba's,' came the reply. 'On whose authority do you, Wilfred, speak?' he asked. 'St. Peter's,' came the reply. 'Well,' said the King, who was no fool, 'I know that when I die St Peter will be the keeper of the Keys of the Kingdom of Heaven, so I vote for Peter and the Roman calculation.'

The political pair looked thoughtful. I wonder if that was on a Thursday, said one of them. But I thought Easter was a pagan festival, said the other. It was, I replied, as you should know. The Festival of Easter, or Oster, was a pagan festival of the spring in honour of Ostara, the Anglo-Saxon Goddess of the spring. The word Easter originally meant Rising – not as in Dublin but as in Lancashire. In fact, in your constituency, if I am not mistaken. And in mine, said the other, in Durham, in the villages. So you must have seen the tomfoolery, I said. On Easter Monday the young men of the village hoist the young maidens aloft and carry them, giggling, through the streets. On Tuesday the girls get their own back. They lift the lads, four girls to a fellow, with a leg or an arm each. The ladies of the royal court did it once to King Edward I. He was not amused and did not speak to them for a week – Easter week.

But he, I imagine, never made the mistake of calling Easter Eve, Easter Saturday. Strictly speaking, Easter Saturday is the Saturday after Easter. I don't care what it is called, said the safer of the two, only when it is.

As recently as 1963, I said, the Vatican Council declared itself in favour of fixing the date of Easter, if and when agreement can

189

be reached with the other churches. If and when. They used to believe here in England that the sun dances on Easter Day. If they ever agree on a fixed day for it, the sun probably will.

So will I, said the one who had come out in favour of the last weekend in March. His companion was not persuaded. Too early, he said. I know that Easter Day cannot be a fixed date like Christmas Day, because you can't have Good Friday on a Tuesday. But I think Easter Day should always be on the last Sunday before April 25.

It is, this year, I said. So when should the election be?

They looked at each other and grinned. On a Thursday, they said, when the moon is full.

April 1992

More Than Just
a Post Office

Every week, every other person in Britain goes to the Post Office. Twenty five million of us. I discovered that fact when I was invited to write a film about the Post Office. And it seemed too good a fact not to put first. Of course it is not difficult to go to the Post Office because there are twenty-thousand post offices in Britain, many more than there are branches of the four big banks or of the five biggest building societies. And so there should be, because we have many more reasons for going to the Post Office.

In the counters business, post offices count most, in every sense. Without them, I think it is fair to say, the nation would be at a loss. There are one thousand two hundred Crown post offices. They are the main post offices in the big cities and the commercial centres. And the people who run them tell me that the majority of their customers in 96 per cent of the Crown post offices are served within two or three minutes. They reckon that you wait for much less time in a post office now than you do in a bank or a building society or at a supermarket checkout.

I argued here recently that Britain invented the orderly queue, and the post office people say that they are perfecting it. People go to the post office not simply to buy postage stamps or postal orders, but to complete any one of no fewer than 150 different transactions. And the Crown post offices, the main post offices, are only the half of it, or to be more precise, only a third of it. Two thirds of the Post Office's business takes place over the counters of the sub-post offices. And there are sixteen sub-post offices for every main post office. They are agencies, run by shopkeepers on behalf of the Post Office.

The Post Office itself is undergoing a revolution. Or perhaps it should be called a counter revolution. Half the Crown post offices in the country have already been modernised, with the intention of matching anything in the high street. Where the downtown has become rundown, and the business centre is elsewhere, the main post office, too, has been moved. Though even a whisper that a post office is to be closed, in town or suburb alike, provokes an immediate outcry. And so it should. It is not so much a complaint as a compliment, a reminder from the local people that they cannot do without a post office. There has to be one. Which is why post offices are now to be found in an increasing number of supermarkets and large stores.

But whether the post office is in the high street, the corner shop, or the out of town shopping centre, it now offers much more than its traditional trade. It still gives as well as receives, issuing pensions and social benefits, and in many places bus passes too. It is a two-way trade. The post office is where most people go to purchase a licence to run the car or turn on the television. But nowadays, it seems, customers demand more, not only more things to purchase but more ways of purchasing them. And so more and more post offices have more and more electronic cash registers, electronic stamp vending machines, electronic phone card vendors.

It is a technological world. Though at the sub-post offices people still have time to chat. Before long, I suspect, we shall be able to buy theatre tickets and airline tickets at a post office, though that will require an Act of Parliament. BUT . . . and this is where those who covet the Post Office's business run for cover . . . half the post offices in Britain, ten thousand of them, run at a loss. The loss makers are the country post offices, and they lose £30 million a year. Market forces would dictate that they should all be closed. But that is unthinkable.

The Post Office as a whole makes a profit, and its country customers cannot be discarded. They are often the elderly, and the least mobile members of society. And the Post Office, I was happy to discover, has no intention of letting them down. It knows, better than anyone, that a village post office, preferably in the village shop, is the centre of village life. So it is encouraging members of the staff to become village sub-post masters and shopkeepers.

And where that is not viable, it is developing part-time post offices, community post offices, opening at the times which suit the village customers best. And that, too, is only right and proper. The Post Office is not merely the counting house for ordinary people, it is an emblem of their existence. It is the place where the people proclaim that they are the public. The old lady drawing her pension is reminding the world of her existence.

That, I think, is the true definition of the public sector. It is a social responsibility, not just a business opportunity.

And that is what counts.

May 1992

Transport of
Delight

The past is its own defence. That thought struck me afresh a
few years ago when I was making a television programme
about the history and the restoration of the canals in this country.
I had just discovered that my great-great-grandfather had been a
lock-keeper, a night lock-keeper no less, on the Grand Union
Canal, and I was eager to discover where he had worked and
what he had done.

I swiftly found myself sharing the enthusiasm of the canal
enthusiasts. It was they who persuaded me that yesterday's
eyesore is tomorrow's preservation order. As one of them put it:
when the first navvies cut the first sods the discriminating averted
their eyes from such a desecration of the landscape. Now they
join working parties to shovel the silt.

And, indeed, I quickly discovered that today the canals and
their trappings are objects of preservation, veneration, and
inspiration – transport of a sylvan age. Today it is leisure and
pleasure; yesterday it was work.

The canals were built to carry coal. They were the first means
devised for moving huge quantities of goods across the country.
And wherever there is a canal somebody is sure to tell you that
that was where the Canal Age began. In truth, as every schoolboy
in Northern Ireland will tell you, Britain's first truly long
distance canal with locks was the Newry Canal in Ulster, which
opened in 1742.

The first in Britain, the St Helen's Canal, better known as
Sankey Brook, followed fifteen years later. But two years after
that, work began on what I believe is the most famous canal of
them all – the one which captured the public's imagination. This
was the Bridgewater Canal, built by James Brindley to carry the

coal from the Duke of Bridgewater's mines at Worsley to Manchester. A canal enthusiast of the time wrote: Gentlemen come to see our eighth wonder of the world – the subterraneous navigation, which is cutting by the great Mr. Brindley, who handles rocks as easily as you would plum pies, and makes the four elements subservient to his will.

The Bridgewater Canal made the Duke a very rich man. But then inland navigation was the road to industrial prosperity, if I may mix a metaphor. Everybody with a pound in his pocket wanted a piece of the action. Canal companies were floated hither and thither, and by the 1830s there was a great network of inland waterways.

I suppose the motorways are the equivalent undertaking in our age, though our ancestors actually built more miles of canal than we have built miles of motorway, so far. Then the speculators began to direct their funds towards the new railways and the canals began to fall into disuse. I think it is fair to argue that the Canal Age began in Britain with the opening of the Bridgewater Canal in 1761, and ended with the opening of the Manchester Ship Canal in 1894. Brindley had carried the Bridgewater over the River Irwell with an astounding stone aqueduct. The engineers of the Ship Canal replaced it with an even more ingenious swinging aqueduct.

It can be argued that the Manchester Ship Canal was the inspiration of a new wide-canal age on the continent, but that is another story. In Britain, for the best part of a century the canals were neglected, but in the last twenty-five years there has been a great activity of restoration.

My favourite, simply because I live near it, is the Cheshire Ring. It embraces sections of no fewer than six canals – the Ashton, the Peak Forest, the Macclesfield, the Trent and Mersey, the Bridgewater and the Rochdale. There is a very beautiful section of the Peak Forest Canal from the foot of Marple Locks – all sixteen of them – to Whaley Bridge. But even more beautiful, I believe, is the stretch of the Macclesfield Canal from Marple to Bosley Locks and on to Mow Cop. Thomas Telford designed this waterway and I think it was his best work. But then I would think that.

For real adventure, many canal enthusiasts argue that the Leeds and Liverpool Canal is the one to explore. They describe it as Britain's longest, most successful, and most important canal. It runs from Liverpool to Wigan, Blackburn, Burnley, Bradford and Leeds. It is the only remaining trans-Pennine waterway and it climbs through magnificent moorland.

In recent years, more and more people have taken to the canals – in every sense. For many of them it is more than a pastime, it is a passion. To the true enthusiast the canals are the best introduction to the landscape, the best approach to geography and history.

I wonder if my great-great-grandfather would agree. If you are on the Grand Union Canal late at night and you bump into his ghost, be sure to ask him.

June 1992

On the Water
Affront

L iving, as I do, on the damp side of the Pennines, I had not,
I must confess, paid much attention to reports of a water
shortage in other parts of England. Until I bumped into an
aggrieved pilgrim. He had gone to visit the Shrine at Walsingham
in Norfolk only to discover that the Holy Water was rationed. It
is enough to turn you into an unbeliever, he said.

You should have prayed for rain, I suggested. But he was not
to be comforted. I am not even allowed to water my own garden,
he complained. Not this year. He was clearly not pleased. Water,
he said, is the miracle on tap, the source of life which in this
green and pleasant land we expect in abundance. And what have
we got? The longest drought on record since 1745.

Not everywhere in England, I said. Not where I live.

Lucky you, he said. Where we are, south of the Wash, the
drought has been steadily worsening for these last four years.
The seven months from September last year to March this year
were the driest this century.

The towns and villages built on the chalkland of East Anglia
have suffered most with things in a zone stretching from Bury
St. Edmunds to Norwich and Cambridge uniquely bad.

I suppose it will be of little comfort, I said, if I tell you that
the fierce drought in the South and East has been accompanied
by heavier than normal rains in the North and West. None at all,
he said. And what makes it worse is that it was entirely
unexpected. It began four years ago, in August 1988, after a
decade of record rainfall. Since then, in our area, water levels are
the lowest ever recorded. Stretches of river have ceased to flow,
and ponds and lakes have dried up. And you know, low rainfall
is not the only problem. The long hot summers of 1989 and 1990

created record rates of evaporation of water from soils in East Anglia and some of the farms are like dust bowls.

So water will have to be rationed, I said.

Yes, but that is not as easy as it sounds. I complain when I am not allowed to water my garden, but now they are talking of banning the irrigation of farmland, as if the farmers haven't enough to worry about. The real problem is that as the level of water goes down, the demand for it goes up. The drier it is the more people require water. The pollution, too, is worsened by the lack of rain. Many sub-standard sewage works discharge their effluent into streams and rivers relying on the flow to dilute it. Undiluted, the sewage flow can wipe out all the wildlife in the water because the bacteria in the sewage consume all the oxygen. My grandson, who is seven, told me that.

So what does he think should be done about the shortage of water? I asked. Your grandson, I mean.

Well, his teacher told him about the plans in the Middle East desert regions to tow icebergs from the Antarctic, so he thinks we should tow icebergs from the Arctic. He can't wait to see one.

And what do you think? I said.

I am an engineer, as you know, he said, and I think it is high time we had a National Water Grid, so the rain that falls on your garden can water mine.

But that would cost a fortune, I said.

True, but something will have to be done. Because we built a large number of dams in the Sixties and early Seventies, we dozed off. Now that we have woken up to the problem we need an engineering solution because we have ignored demand control. I think we should use the canals to transfer water from one part of the country to another. They are already in place and with some pumping and engineering to get rid of the bottlenecks we could move large amounts of water to the areas of greatest need. Canals are cheaper than pipelines because you just pump the water around the lock system rather than fight against the friction of a pipe.

The friction of a pipe, I echoed. I bet your grandson told you that too.

He did, and he is right.

So where could the water come from and go to?

Well, one option would be to extract water in the Severn Trent region, transfer it to the Trent and Mersey Canal near Stafford, and then send it on its way. Perhaps into the Grand Union Canal and the Oxford Canal to serve the Thames region, then on into the River Ouse and the Nene in the Anglian Water region.

What about Kielder reservoir in Northumberland, the largest man-made lake in Europe?

Perfect, he said. It could send millions of gallons of surplus water a day into the River Ouse and then on to Lincolnshire, Suffolk, and Essex.

Would that not be very expensive? I said.

Indeed it would be, he said, but it will have to be done. If, as we suspect, the South East of England becomes drier and warmer, the problems of water supply will be much greater than those of water demand.

He paused, for effect. This is a national priority, he said. In that case, I replied, we need a Minister for Water.

He grinned. Precisely, he said. The ideal job for a Tory Wet.

July/August 1992

The World
at War

Forty years ago we were students together, reading history. After university our ways parted. He went into teaching, I into journalism. We seldom meet now, but when we do it is always on the Manchester-London train. Invariably I am reading newspapers and he is marking exam papers. But on this occasion he was setting an exam paper. How about this for a question, he said? The Third World War began in June 1992. Discuss.

I looked at him in alarm, and then the penny dropped. The Second World War, I said, began in April 1932. Discuss. And we both laughed, because that was the question we had been set in 1952. And we had been able to tackle it because we had both heard A. J. P. Taylor lecture on the subject.

Taylor argued, and subsequently put all his arguments in a famous book, that if a formal declaration of war marks the starting point, then the Second World War began in April 1932 when Mao Tse-Tung and Chou Teh declared war against Japan in the name of the Kiangsi Soviet. Many historians, he said, conditioned to think of Europe as the centre of the world, date the Second World War from September 1, 1939, when Germany attacked Poland. But that is not an answer which would satisfy the Abyssinians or the Chinese for whom the war began earlier, nor the Russians or the Americans for whom the war began later. Indeed he said, I remember, that if we wait until the war was being fought in every continent except the two Americas, the date was 1942, or even 1944.

Taylor's essential point was that the Second World War was not an immediate global conflict in which East declared war on West, or North on South, but a number of small wars which gradually coalesced into a great one. And even then they did not coalesce fully. The very title World War was bestowed on the 1914-18 War only in retrospect. At the time people simply called it the Great War.

The Second World War was not only 'Greater' in the sense that it spread across a greater part of the globe, but very different. The First World War was fought throughout in much the same place and in much the same way. The Second World War repeatedly changed both its locations and its character as it wore on.

The nature of the First World War is not difficult to define. It was a conflict between two alliances – the Triple Entente (France, Great Britain, Russia) on one side, and the Central Powers (Austria-Hungary and Germany) on the other. The war was within a single society. It aroused simple passions. In 1914 excited public opinion pushed the governments towards war.

But that was not true of the Second World War. The statesmen led and the people followed. A. J. P. Taylor, I remember, argued that in the First World War the popular heroes were the generals, but in the Second World War the generals were administrators. Only the political leaders counted. Four men, he said, made every important decision of the war personally – Hitler, Churchill, Roosevelt and Stalin. Only Japan was run by an almost anonymous committee. But Taylor also believed that in spite of the killing and the destruction which accompanied it, the Second World War was a good war in that it was fought to liberate people from Nazi – and, to a lesser extent, Japanese – tyranny, and it succeeded. Though it did leave a large part of the world under the tyranny of Communism.

All this we were discussing with the enthusiasm of youthful recollection, when I reminded my old friend that it is easy to be wise after the event. Historians can impose upon past events a pattern which was not visible to those who attended upon the events. I take it, I said, that the events of June 1992 which provoked your exam question were the conflicts in Bosnia and Moldova and the decision to cut Czechoslovakia in two.

Plus the assassination of the President of Algiers and the massacre in South Africa, he said. And he went on to discuss the various forces provoking conflict – nationalism, fundamentalism, racism, despair. War, he said, quoting a famous war historian, is both an accepted and an acceptable part of human behaviour.

At that point we reached our destination. That is still no excuse, I said, for leaping to conclusions. We went our separate ways. He to a meeting of an examining board, I to my London flat. And there among the post was a new book, sent by the publishers, and entitled *Future Wars*.* It discussed who will fight them and why. Where and how they will be fought. Who will win.

It was not history but a forecast. It argued that in the coming decade the world will almost certainly witness a number of large-scale conventional wars. It even listed them: The Russian Civil War, The Second Korean War, The Third Gulf War, the Fourth India-Pakistan War, the Sixth Arab-Israeli War. But, thank goodness, no mention of a Third World War. Which, I suppose, is some comfort.

September 1992

* *Future Wars* by Trevor Dupuy is published by Sidgwick and Jackson, price £17.50.

202

Make My
Day

M ichaelmas is not what it was.

Once upon a time on Michaelmas Day – September 29, the Feast of St Michael and All Angels – everybody had a goose for dinner.

At Christmas a capon, at Michaelmas a goose,
And somewhat else at New Year's tide for fear the lease flies
loose.

Tenants would recite that rhyme when they presented their landlord with a goose to keep in his graces.

Michaelmas Day was one of the Quarter Days, when rents were due, and magistrates were chosen.

It was long believed that Queen Elizabeth 1, on her way to Tilbury Fort on September 29, 1588, dined with Sir Neville Umfreyville, and partook of goose, afterwards calling for a bumper of Burgundy, and giving as a toast: 'Death to the Spanish Armada!'

Scarcely had she spoken when a messenger announced the destruction of the Spanish Fleet by storm, The Queen demanded a second bumper, and said: 'Henceforth shall a goose commemorate this great victory.'

And henceforth it did, until some spoilsport historian pointed out that there was not a word of truth in the story. The Spanish Armada was dispersed by storm winds in July, 1588, and the Thanksgiving sermon for victory was preached in St Paul's Cathedral on August 20, 1588, almost six weeks before Michaelmas.

But goose or no goose, Michaelmas Day, September 29, was long celebrated as the first day; in the older universities, the autumn term is still called the Michaelmas Term.

But I think we should make even more of Michaelmas. And I was seized of that thought on Michaelmas Day last year, when it fell on a Sunday, and I found myself throwing the switch to floodlight the Town Hall at New Mills.

New Mills is in the High Peak District of Derbyshire, where Derbyshire, Cheshire, and Manchester meet.

The reason for the ceremony last year was to celebrate six hundred years. Documentary evidence had just come to light which revealed the existence of the corn mill – later the 'New Mill' – in Michaelmas, 1391.

New Mills is a town everyone should visit, though not all at once. It is a unique blend of natural history and industrial history. It is the town with The Park Under The Town.

Let me explain what that means.

New Mills is perched above the Torrs, rocky gorges where two rivers, the Goyt and the Sett, meet before flowing on into the Mersey. Six hundred years ago, as we now know, the fast flowing water turned the wheels of corn mills. Two hundred years ago the water turned the wheels of cotton mills.

The Torrs were excellent sites for cotton mills, because the mills could be built on a rocky terrace a few feet above the water.

And they were. The mills multiplied and the town prospered. A canal was cut, the railways came, and more than thirty bridges were built.

But then the bad times came.

Now all this is a familiar story in cotton towns. Old mills have to be demolished; new industry wooed.

But the people of New Mills were very much aware that the Torrs, even strewn with ruined mills, is still a beautiful place. So they hit upon the idea of making it a Country Park under the Town, a Riverside Park, a Heritage Trail.

And they have made a beautiful job of it.

Everyone whom I have persuaded to visit it has been overjoyed. An American friend said that it was the best combination imaginable of a country walk and a historic tour.

And the local people are taking a greater and greater interest in the town's history.

Which brings me back to Michaelmas Day. For it was on that day last year, talking to people in New Mills about the history of the town, that made me think that this was an excellent way to celebrate Michaelmas.

I have argued here before that we have made a mess of May, imposing upon it two nondescript Bank Holidays three weeks apart, and neglecting Whitsun.

Instead, I think, we should abolish the two Monday holidays in May, May Day and the Spring Bank Holiday, and make Michaelmas Day a public holiday.

St Michael, I am sure, would approve. He is usually depicted as an archangel in full armour, with a sword and a pair of scales, and piercing a dragon or a devil with his lance.

Michaelmas Day could then be the day on which we revere the past. Which is very appropriate because Michaelmas Day is almost certainly the anniversary of the dedication of a church of St Michael and All Angels on the Salarian Way in Rome in the sixth century.

And nothing adds more to the enjoyment of where you live than knowledge of its history.

That is true for the young as well as the old. But it was an elderly lady in New Mills who put it all in one sentence.

Brian, she said, I never knew I lived in such an interesting place.

October 1992

Charity Begins
at Home

In this country we are great givers to charity. We may not be the greatest creators of wealth in the world, but we are generous with what we have. We are almost always first to respond to appeals to feed and clothe the hungry in countries stricken by famine. And at home we have a very clear list of priorities:

Number 1: cancer. We give more to cancer charities than to anything else.
Number 2: physical handicap.
Number 3: children in need.
Number 4: animals, especially cats (and rightly so).
Number 5: the elderly. (Pause for applause.)

I know all this to be true from my own limited experience of fund-raising. You have only to say hospice and people give because they value the work of the hospice in their community. I first made an appeal on behalf of a hospice when there were only two in Britain. Now there are 152, and every one is generously supported.

But for some good causes, even in this generous country, it is not enough to hold out a collection box and say 'Please', you have to argue the case. We dig fairly deeply into our pockets and purses to fund research into heart disease, but we are less than generous when it comes to contributing to mental health charities. Why is that?

It cannot be that we do not believe that there is a problem. Of the 20 million people who consult their doctors every year, at least one in four is treated for an identifiable psychiatric disorder.

And that number is increasing. Perhaps we are reluctant to face up to the truth. It is one thing to say airily. 'I think I am going round the bend', and quite another to observe that your friend or your neighbour or your loved one has.

Though we are not as stupid about it as we used to be. My grandmother, my mother's mother, worked as a nurse in a 'lunatic asylum' at the turn of the century, and she used to tell me stories about what went on in there which put me off Victorian values for the rest of my life. We are better now. We all understand that mankind is not divided between US, the normal ones, and THEM, the disturbed ones.

We now realise that it can happen to any of us, even if we are sometimes reluctant to admit that certain behaviour is a mental disorder: anorexia, for example, alcoholism, excessive grief at a time of bereavement.

That is when people need help. But there are also afflictions where the afflicted are dismissed by some as having only themselves to blame. The homeless, for example. A few may be foolhardy but most of them are the hapless victims of circumstance. Things have gone wrong for them and they have nowhere to live. They doss down where they can, in town and country, trapped in their predicament. They cannot get work because employers, even if they have vacancies, do not like to take on people of no fixed abode. And without work, the homeless cannot raise the money for a roof over their heads.

A year ago I was invited to appeal for funds for a charity which helps the homeless, and I was astonished by the scale of the problem. The number with nowhere to live was equal to the population of a whole town, a growing town. I discovered that homelessness was not just a crisis at Christmas, but a crisis all the year round and all round Britain. And yet homelessness is a misfortune which can be alleviated, given the will and the money. But, at a time of recession, what can be done to help the unemployed, especially for the young, to find work?

Nearly one in three teenagers is out of work, and it does seem especially unfair because they are too young to be blamed for the recession, and not to have a job is a rotten start to adult life. One charity I know came to the assistance of a boy called Stephen who hit upon the idea of leaving school at Easter, instead of waiting until July, so that he would be applying for jobs before his contemporaries came on to the market.

He decided that he would job-hunt by day, swot at night, and hope to start work the moment he had finished his exams. There was only one problem; he had no money and he did not want to sponge off his mother. He was in fact entitled to a small contribution from the State, and with the help of the charity he got enough money to pay the fares for his interviews, to buy a new shirt, and to give his mother something for his keep.

You will be delighted to know that he found a job and he passed his exams. And the charity which helped him is helping many other young people to find work. In truth there are very few misfortunes which afflict people in this country that some charity is not seeking to correct.

I was much taken by the work of one in particular which helps grandparents whose grandchildren are in care. I had not realised that some grandparents are denied the opportunity of seeing their grandchildren at Christmas, not because they live at the other end of the world, or because they are too frail, but simply because they are not allowed to.

Their grandchildren are in care, not because of abuse or neglect, but for a variety of reasons including family sickness, bad housing, poverty, and other misfortunes. Those who cannot live with their parents do best when placed with grandparents, and if that is not possible, continuing contact with grandparents is good for those placed in the care of non-relatives. But some local authorities forbid such contact. Or did, until the charity took up the cause.

And now they will be home together at Christmas, which is where charity begins.

November/December 1992

High Days
and Holidays

Nineteen ninety-three will be the International Year of: a. the Acorn, b. the Axiom, c. the Conker, d. the Concept, e. the Perimeter, f. the Parameter.

Or perhaps not. But one thing is sure. Some pressure group or other will annexe the year and claim it as its own. Someone always does.

Years have a fascination for mankind. We measure our own lives in them, though at school, I recall, we had one bright spark in our class who, whenever he was asked his age, always gave it in days. If he is still alive he must now be 22,645, or thereabouts. His precision was not simply affectation. He had a very good reason for calculating his age by the day: his birthday was February 29th.

He was much given, I remember, to reminding the teacher that a natural year is precisely 365 days, five hours forty-eight minutes and forty-six seconds. Though even he was momentarily confounded when our Sunday School teacher told us about the Year of Confusion. That was A.D. 46, the year in which the Julian calendar was introduced, and it lasted for no fewer than 445 days.

Some people have enough difficulty counting to one hundred. Indeed I lost count of the number of letters I received when I happened to say on the radio one morning that A.D. 2000 is not the first year of the 21st century, but the last year of the 20th.

Prove it, demanded countless correspondents. Ask any cricketer, I replied, he will tell you that ninety-nine is not a century. This century still has eight years to go.

I have argued here before, on more than one occasion, that we have made a mess of May. To have two Bank Holidays in the same month, one on the first Monday and one on the last never made sense. In 1992 they were only three weeks apart. And 1993 is precisely the year to cancel both the May Bank Holiday and the Spring Bank Holiday and to celebrate Whit instead.

It can be achieved without changing the calendar. Easter Sunday, as you know, can never be earlier than March 22 and never later than April 25. In 1993 it falls on April 11. Whit Sunday, Pentecost, is seven weeks after Easter Day, so in 1993 it falls on May 30. But there are thirty-one days in May, and that means that in 1993 Whit Monday is both the last Monday in the month as well as the last day in the month. So that day is already designated the Spring Bank Holiday. Let us therefore celebrate it as Whit Monday and insist that it is the Bank Holiday hereafter.

It will sometimes be the last Monday in May, but not often. Because it is always seven weeks after Easter, it can be as early as May 11 or as late as June 14. But the seven-week gap makes sense. It is the right rhythm of the calendar. In these last fifteen years when we have had two May Bank Holidays a very late Easter has meant that we could have three Bank Holiday Mondays in five weeks. Crazy.

So, let me repeat, from 1993 onwards we should abandon both the May Day Bank Holiday and the Spring Bank Holiday and restore Whit Monday as a Bank Holiday.

And that means that we are owed one.

I suggested here once before that we could celebrate Ascension Day which is always a Thursday, forty days after Easter and ten days before Whit Sunday. But lots of *Saga* magazine readers wrote to me saying that was as daft as having two Bank Holidays in May. Too close together.

Some argued that it would make more sense to extend the Whitsun holiday, having the Friday as well as the Monday. But some wanted the Friday before, and some the Friday after.

Only a few weeks ago, after I had written here about Michaelmas Day, September 29, a reader in <u>Rutland</u> (which he underlined) said that he agreed that Michaelmas should be a public holiday, but only if we reverted in England to the proper August Bank Holiday at the beginning of that month, and abandoned the Late Summer Holiday at the end of that month.

What is abundantly clear from the correspondence is that public holidays are a matter which engage public attention, even among those no longer at work. Some favour celebrating famous victories, the Battle of Trafalgar, the Battle of Waterloo. Some favour celebrating acts of discovery or exploration, the Ascent of Everest, the Journey to the Pole. A few wags favour Guy Fawkes Day. After all, said one, it is the most famous day in our history.

January 1993

Towards the
Universal City

I t was a lively meeting. It had been advertised as a symposium
on Town AND Country, but it rapidly became an argument
about Town VERSUS Country. As chairman, impartial as ever,
I had opened the proceedings by reminding everyone present
that ours is a country of 56 million acres, inhabited by 56 million
people.

That, I said, is one each. Though some people have rather
more than their share.

The big landowner present grimaced.

Then I got to the point.

In the first half of this century, I said, reciting my favourite
statistic, we built on as much land as we had in the whole of our
previous history. I paused to let the point sink in. And a man at
the back of the hall immediately capped it.

If things go on as they are, he said, in the hundred years from
1945 to 2045 we shall have built on as much land again as we had
in the whole of our previous history.

In these hundred years, he continued, the countryside built
on, or, as they say, developed, will be an area larger than the
counties of Durham, Dorset, Bedfordshire, Derbyshire, Hertfordshire, and Warwickshire combined. In fact, he said, by 2075
the total urban area in England will equal eighteen Greater
Londons.

The audience was aghast. Even the few developers present
seemed taken aback. One after another, people got up to argue
that it must not be allowed to happen. But they were less certain
about how to prevent it. It is not enough, said one, for us to
behave like the Mad Hatter and simply chant: No room, no
room.

Some argued that all future building development should be re-development, the re-use of land previously built on. I remembered that I had once suggested to a Secretary of State for the Environment that all inner city derelict land should be re-designated Green Belt. Then, I argued, the developers would cajole the chairmen of Planning Committees into granting them permission to build on it. The developers were not amused.

One man argued that all future housing development should be high-rise, a remark which provoked a series of anecdotes about the follies of the 1960s, when the planners thought they knew best.

An academic among us pointed out that research had shown that high-rise dwellings need so much space around them that the density of population is actually lower than in terraced housing. And people much prefer to live close to the ground.

Then I remembered Doctor Doxiadis.

He was an ekistician (ekistics is the science of human settlement), whom I interviewed for half-an-hour thirty years ago. I have never forgotten what he said. He was an Athenian and he told me that Athens grows by eighteen dwellings an hour. As we had been talking, nine buildings had gone up.

He then went on to argue that our cities have gone wrong because they have grown too much in the wrong direction. The values which had been created in the human habitat around people in the past have been lost.

A city of the past, he said, had a total length of a mile and a half so it took little more than twenty minutes to walk from one side to the other. But the city of the present has to contain not a maximum of fifty thousand people but 5 millions or more. And that requires a length of fifty miles.

What we must do, he said, is to divide present-day cities into small units within which we can establish all the human values of the past. I want, he said, as every one does, to live in a house with a small garden around it, in a neighbourhood, as they did in fifth century Athens.

I want, he said, to live on a human scale.

I then asked him, I recall, if a city should not be like a bicycle wheel with a fixed hub and with longer and longer spokes, but more like a stick of rock, with the name running right through the middle.

213

This was his reply. You must remember that he was broadcasting on Radio 3. The answer, he said, is a parabolic city. You start with a small city, like a small bicycle wheel. But instead of letting the city grow all around into a larger and larger wheel, you must think of the centre of the wheel moving in one direction continually producing a new city around the moving centre.

A one-directional growth of the centre, he said, gives you the chance to let the old centre survive until all its economic and cultural values are amortised.

I looked puzzled, I remember. Paid off, he explained.

And so, he said, you have the original city centre, and next to it you have the centre of fifty years later, and next to it the centre fifty years later again. So if you have a city which is five hundred years old, you have the full evolution of its centre and of the residential areas around it.

The city grows into time. No part of it is abandoned, and the citizens can live in and around the centre they love best.

But would there not be a danger, I asked him, of a city growing right across a country from coast to coast?

Yes, he replied. We are moving towards the universal city, the ecumenic city. We shall build continuous corridors of cities. I reckon, he said, that a century from now, the principal city of England will start in Liverpool and Manchester, come down to London, reach across to the Netherlands, travel along the Rhine, and down to Milan.

All this, I attempted to explain to the symposium.

There was silence, as people struggled to imagine what this universal city would be like.

Finally an old woman, who was sitting in the front row, spoke. I had a different vision, she said, of the celestial city.

February 1993

All in the Same Bus

The old lady at the bus-stop was livid.

Late again, she said.

The bus? I asked, innocently.

No, you fool, she said. Me. The only other person at the bus-stop, a smartly dressed middle-aged man, looked at his watch.

If we were ever to miss the bus, he said solemnly, we would have only ourselves to blame.

Explain yourself, I said.

He escorted us back into the bus-shelter and held forth.

The bus, he said, is the universal passenger transport of the modern world and we cannot do without it.

You can't say we haven't tried. There was a time when you could take a bus from almost anywhere to almost anywhere at almost anytime.

But not now.

Now you might have to wait, or even wait in vain. But you ought not to have to wait much longer.

The old lady looked relieved. And a crowd began to gather round the shelter.

In a world of diminishing oil resources, said the speaker, the bus is the unselfish use of fuel oil for road passenger transport. It makes the oil go further, and we with it.

Buses take children to school, housewives to market, the world to work. Whenever and wherever the bus is given the chance to show what it can do, it does it well. And if the buses had the roads to themselves, think what they could achieve.

One bus with fifty passengers where previously fifty cars snarled in the tangled traffic, consuming fuel, emitting fumes, blocking each other's path. But sadly, he went on, the buses do not have it all to themselves. The authorities still clear a lane, reserve a road, allow a turn, but not much more.

Not yet.

And often when they do attempt to untangle the traffic and impose a one-way system, it takes the bus the wrong way round, the long way round, and the passengers have to pay more. Because the rule of the road is that the size of the fare is equal to the distance travelled.

He warmed to this theme.

This was clearly a performance.

Buses have to make their own way in this world, he said. And yet no one seriously doubts that if the bus were given its head, if it were allowed priority on the public highway, then its service would be unfailingly prompt, regular, frequent, and – most important of all – precise.

Because what matters most is that a bus should go where and when and as often as its passengers desire.

It must serve them, not they it.

The old lady nodded in agreement.

And equally, he said, no one can dispute that the bus should be the priority customer for fuel oil. Fifty men in a Clapham omnibus consume much less fuel per passenger mile than one man at the wheel of a private car. Other countries think better of the bus than we do. They give it more resources, more support, more priority. They talk not of subsidy but of investment, not of reduction but of expansion.

They know that the bus is the least expensive and the most economical, the safest and the most sensible, method of carrying the bulk of the people precisely to where they want to go.

They know that it is folly to impede the bus, to limit its operation, to deny it access. They know that when all the factors are honestly assessed – cost, care, convenience, conservation – the bus is best.

We can no longer afford to wait for the bus, nor dare we miss it. The days when each of us can have an internal combustion engine are drawing to a close. We have neither the fuel nor the space. We must learn to share, because we are all in the same bus.

At that very moment a bus drew up at the bus-stop. All aboard, said the old lady, leading the way.

I could not resist asking one question of the man who had been holding forth. Are you, I asked, the local Member of Parliament?

I was, he replied. But I lost my seat at the last election.

March 1993

Time and
Motion Study

Three days a week I get up at half past four in the morning and a cab picks me up at ten to five to take me to work. But one morning recently the cab arrived at a quarter past four. I was not amused. Neither was the cab driver. And when I finally got into his cab he had no doubt who and what was to blame.

It is that ridiculous twenty-four-hour clock, he said. Whoever booked the cab said 0-four-fifty, and it was misheard as 0-four-fifteen. They should have said ten to five. I agreed. And then he went on to denounce all the conversions of measurement – length, volume, weight, and temperature.

When I set out for somewhere, he said, I want to know how many miles it is, not how many kilometres. When I am looking for an address I want to know how many yards down the street it is, not how many metres. When I am looking for something small I want to know how many feet long it is, not how many centimetres. When it rains heavily I want to know how many inches of rain fell, not how many millimetres.

When I see a field I want to know how many acres it is, not how many hectares. When I fill up the cab I want to know how many gallons I have put in, not how many litres. And I like to buy oil, like beer, in pints. When I buy groceries I want to know how many pounds in weight, not how many kilograms. And when I am behind a lorry I want to know how many tons it is carrying, not how many tonnes.

Pardon, I said.

You know, he said, the one that looks like a misspelling.

By this time I had my pocket diary open. Our ton is heavier, I said, it is equal to 1.016 of their tonnes. But he was not to be interrupted. The weather men are the worst, he said. When it is

218

going to be a hot day I want to know if it is going to be in the sixties or the seventies. When it is going to be a cold day I want to know how many degrees of frost. And I mean Fahrenheit not Centigrade.

And who is this Celsius?

Anders Celsius, I replied, a Swedish astronomer. In 1742 he devised the Centigrade thermometer and the temperature scale named after him.

I was reading from the diary.

And did you know, I said, that thirty miles an hour is equal to forty-eight kilometres an hour?

No I did not, he replied, but I know how fast I'm going. And that's another thing. People cannot even agree on how to pronounce the word. Some say kill-ometre and some say killometre.

He pulled up because we had reached my destination.

How much on the clock? I asked.

Four fifty, he replied.

You mean four pounds ten shillings, I said.

He grinned and grabbed the last word.

We should never have gone decimal, he said, it devalued our money.

I remembered his words that afternoon when I bought an evening newspaper, which used to cost a penny and now costs six shillings.

And almost everyone of my generation to whom I have mentioned my encounter with the cab driver has agreed with him.

We have grown accustomed to the decimal currency, but many of us still think fondly of shillings and pence. And there is no doubt that we prefer feet and inches to any metric measurement.

If we ever reach the last mile there will be uproar.

Many people are adept at converting Centigrade to Fahrenheit. Double it, subtract ten per cent, and add thirty-two.

At the garage old customers think in gallons and regard litres as a device for pretending that petrol is cheaper than it is. Good cooks, who are old cooks, measure in pounds and ounces. Grandfathers expect their grandsons to run a hundred yards not a hundred metres. No old farmer has a kind word for the hectare. And no one of our age, repeat no one, would dream of announcing that he or she is going to bed at twenty-three hundred hours.

I think it is time we put the clock back.

April 1993

One Track
Mind

S he had one in each hand. This, she said, raising her left
hand, is my bus pass. This, she said, raising her right hand,
is my Senior Railcard. And I need them both.

Then I recognised her.

We met at a bus-stop, I said, a couple of months ago. What
are you doing here at Euston?

Going to Glasgow, she said, to see my grandchildren. She
glanced up at the time. I must go, she said. Be sure to tell the
editor of *Saga* magazine that I support his campaign to preserve
easy rail access for the elderly.

And off she went to catch the Glasgow train. While I, as usual
on a Thursday morning, boarded the Macclesfield train, thinking, for the umpteenth time, how much easier it is to go home
by train.

It is true that as a Founder Friend of the M6 I have
frequently endorsed the economic benefits of motorways.
And I have lost count of the number of transport ministers
whom I have sought to persuade to introduce an integrated
transport policy. The wheels of the economy need road and
rail.

When Dr Beeching set out to prune the railways, egged on by
Ernie Marples, the first line he chose to close was from Newcastle-upon-Tyne to Washington, County Durham (or, as we
now say, Tyne and Wear). The following week the government,
of which Mr Marples was a member, announced that Washington
would be the site of the next New Town in Britain.

The truth is that we never know when we are going to need a
railway again, which is why it is daft to close even little lines.
When BBC television broadcast its famous series, Great Railway

Journeys of the World, I made a local television programme about the one they forgot: Stockport to Stalybridge.

It is a seven-and-a-half-mile industrial adventure, starting from the biggest brick-built bridge in the world and ending at the finest railway buffet in the land. No one, I hope, would dare close that. And it is a short cut from one Inter-City line to another.

People moan about Inter-City trains running late. And even the Macclesfield train has been known to be late, though not often. But good time-keeping is not the reason I choose to travel by train. I regard that as the driver's concern. For me the train is both a means of getting there and a means of getting away from it all.

Some train travellers hanker for telephone connections and secretarial services aboard; but not me. I settle back in the seat happy not to be interrupted. A train journey is a chance to read and to think and to sleep, with a bite to eat when I am feeling hungry and a drink when I am thirsty.

I have a friend who says that he does all his serious reading on trains. It is the only place where he is undisturbed. I asked him once if he had noticed that the class of book read is the opposite of the class travelled. First class passengers read second class literature, and vice versa.

On a visit to the buffet bar I pointed out to him that those passengers in first class were reading Jeffrey Archer and the like, and those in standard class, Gabriel Garcia Marquez and the like.

They are students, he said. And he was just about to complain about the noise leaking from the headphones of a student listening to a personal radio, when his cell phone rang.

Do what they all do, I said, and say: anything in the post, Fiona, darling?

After that he switched off the cell phone and we settled down to a quiet talk about the future of the railways. He, like me, thinks that trains make travelling a pleasure. But he also believes that a train journey is not just a journey from A to B with only the destination important.

He says that it is a trip along a track with every inch exclusive to the purpose. Every motor vehicle can have access to a road but only a train can use a railway. He thinks it would be silly to

222

have all that track – all those embankments and viaducts and stations and signal boxes – and no trains.

And he gets very cross about the small amount of money we spend on the railways, compared to France and Germany.

They know, he said once, that rail travel is both the journey done and the distance travelled.

I nodded in agreement.

And then I reminded him of the time when British Rail ran the slogan: this is the age of the train. And some joker scribbled on the poster at Euston: ours is 103.

I said then, and I still think, that their slogan should simply be: The Permanent Way.

May 1993

Strike up the Band

We got the idea from the Saracens during the Crusades. They had bands to inspire their forces and we took up the idea.

The speaker was a young officer in the Royal Northumberland Fusiliers. The place was Fenham Barracks, Newcastle-upon-Tyne. The year was 1950. The time was two o'clock in the morning. And I was on guard duty.

I had been in the Army, on national service, all of three weeks. Guard duty was part of the initial training, but I was not yet allowed to handle a rifle. So I stood on guard armed with only a pick handle, a sight which provoked much merriment among passers-by.

The officer, who had clearly been out on the tiles, had stopped to ask kindly about the welfare of 22005587 Private Redhead.

Have you, he said, any interests or hobbies?

Yes Sir, I replied. I am fascinated by history and I play the clarinet.

That set him off.

So, he said, you will know that a military band is not a brass band, but a band composed of woodwind, brass and percussion. Clarinets were first introduced about the time of the Seven Years War.

Between 1756 and 1763, I said, showing off.

Yes, he said. And at that time many military bands here in Britain were maintained unofficially at the officers' expense. They were very small. They usually consisted of two clarinets, two oboes, two bassoons, two horns and a drum or two.

But as the bands grew bigger the number of clarinets

increased, and they became, as it were, the violins of the orchestra.

At this point in his peroration, the sergeant of our platoon appeared, and the officer took his salute as the signal to depart.

Talks too much that one, said the sergeant.

But the next day, to my surprise, and I suspect to the sergeant's annoyance, I was marched from the barrack room to the square, not to practise drill, but to witness a rehearsal by the regimental band.

I was not invited to play but I was instructed to sort out the parts, and I was then invited, or more accurately, ordered to accompany the band to Berwick upon Tweed on the following Saturday.

On that Saturday I sat in the lorry with the clarinet players, guarding their parts with my life. Their music, I should perhaps explain, was on small cards which fitted into a special clip on the bell of their clarinets. My task was to make sure that every musician had the right music.

For the parade in Berwick the bandsmen wore full dress uniform, and I watched in awe. Though one lad did stumble when his tall black fur hat slipped over his eyes. The others were still laughing about it when we drove back down the Great North Road.

All this came back to me on that sad day earlier this year when it was announced that the number of military bands in Britain is to be greatly reduced. Not everyone shares my sorrow. Some people see military bands not as part of a glorious heritage but as vainglorious. But the officer who held my attention while I stood to attention would not agree. He, and I am now putting words in his mouth, would argue that regimental bands are not symbols of aggression, displays of arrogance, or military charades. They are a sign of our confidence in the continuity of our history, a reminder.

We are sceptical about sudden breaks, or the need for revolutionary change. We prefer to go from precedent to precedent. And if the sergeant were to interrupt and accuse him of being too philosophical, then I suspect that he would simply argue the case for the music.

He might even quote that wonderfully eccentric English

composer Joseph Holbrooke, who took it into his head to dabble in military bands and was flabbergasted by the possibilities.

Such clarinets, he wrote. Did every Englishman's heart beat at all normally, when the Coldstreams and Grenadiers clarinets have a swing. Ye Gods. Out, ye violins!

And if a man from the Treasury were to put it to him that we simply cannot afford all the military bands because they cost £60 million a year to support, he could always quote the RAF officer, who was reported to have said: 'Sixty million pounds may seem a lot of money to people in the Arts, but it compares favourably with the cost of two Tornados – and we usually crash a couple of them every year.'

Strike up the band.

June 1993

Winning Ways
with Cheese

I n the very same week which witnessed a great argument in
this country about there being too much emphasis on bad
news, I found myself at an event in Geneva which was without
doubt a celebration of good news.

It was the presentation ceremony of the 1993 Rolex Awards
for Enterprise. And I was there, not, I hasten to say, because I
had won an award, but because I had helped to choose the five
winners, or, as Rolex calls them the five laureates.

I, and my fellow members of the Selection Committee, were
spoiled for choice. The Rolex Awards, which are given every
three years, attract literally hundreds of nominations from all
over the world. But they are not simply gestures of international
recognition for achievements already acclaimed. They are much
more original, in every sense of that word.

They are bestowed upon individuals, men and women, who
demonstrate a true spirit of enterprise and orginality in one of
the three following categories: applied science and invention;
exploration and discovery; and the environment. They are a
tribute to the rich diversity of human enterprise, to the ingenuity
and imagination of people.

I found all the entries fascinating because they were all bright
ideas. My favourite philosopher of this century once defined
originality as a matter of taking a hint. To be the first to take the
hint requires not only imagination but determination too, often
in the face of indifference or dissent.

The Rolex Award laureates are all involved in something
which was crying out to be done, but they were the first both to
hear, and to answer, that cry.

In a world worried about the ozone layer and capable of

measuring it only from a handful of very expensive machines Forrest M. Mimms III has invented TOPS.

TOPS is a low-cost hand-held Total Ozone Portable Spectrordiometer capable of calculating the thickness of the ozone layer and the ultraviolet radiation which penetrates down through the atmosphere.

Mimms plans to equip the members of a global ozone measurement network he is organising with this instrument so that they can measure the ozone layer in isolated areas of the world. Then we really will know what is going on around the planet.

Steven Garrett, who is also an American, and a professor of physics, is developing a thermo-acoustic refrigerator, in which cold is generated by sound waves from a loudspeaker. His fridge does not require the chlorofluorocarbons (CFC's) which are used in conventional refrigerators and which threaten the ozone layer. We shall probably all have one soon.

Aldo Lo Curto is an Italian doctor who divides his time between his plastic surgery practice in Italy and what could be called a very specialist general practice among Amazonian Indians.

He has produced a medical handbook for the Indians, simply written, carefully illustrated, and explaining not only the diseases which may afflict them but the cures most easily available, not least among the forest plants. It is an anthology of their knowledge as well as of his, and instantly usable.

Antonio De Vivo is an Italian PE teacher and also one of Italy's leading speleologists (someone who underakes the scientific study of caves). He has already led an expedition which navigated the Rio La Venta in Mexico.

The Rio La Venta is a wild river running along the bottom of a canyon at the foot of very tall, steep cliffs. He plans to return on another expedition not simply to canoe down the river but to explore the cliffs.

He believes that they contain not only mysterious caves as yet unexplored but also the entrance to some long-lost ancient city.

The only woman among the five Rolex laureates this year is Nancy Abeiderrahmane from Mauritania. I had the pleasure at Geneva of presenting her with her award and I chose to introduce her by her maiden name: Nancy Jones.

Nancy is the united nations in herself, the very emblem of

humanity. Her ancestors are Welsh, English, Spanish, German and Russian, and she is married to a Mauritanian.

When she went to live in Nouakchott, the capital of Mauritania, she was surprised by the lack of regular supplies of fresh milk. So she founded a milk processing plant and set up a network of herdsmen in the surrounding desert to provide her plant with a regular supply of cow's milk and camel's milk.

She pasteurises the milk and also produces camel's milk cheese. It is delicious. I know because I ate some.

Her enterprise has not only improved the local economy, it has also made the local people healthier and happier. And her four children are very proud of their mother.

When I presented her with her award the photographers flocked round her.

Say cheese, I said.

July/August 1993

229

A Little of
What You Fancy

I saw only the top of his head. And the hand with the pen in it. 'Would you sign this, Sir,' I said. 'It's rather urgent.' I pushed the paper on to his blotter his way up and he signed. I thanked him and was gone, wobbling hastily down the long hot corridor like an Olympic walker until I reached the safety of the motorcycle outside. I put on my cap and belt and headed back.

I had borrowed the motorcycle that morning to cross the island from Second Echelon to GHQ. I had never ridden one before, nor indeed since, but in spite of running over a snake I managed the journey to get the signature of Brigadier A (for Admin), in the guise of a clerk on his staff.

Now I could go to Australia.

The year was 1949, the month September, and along with countless other National Servicemen I was holding back the Communist threat to Malaya. My own contribution to imperial defence was to play records on Radio Malaya – 'This is Sgt. Brian Redhead introducing the records that YOU have chosen' – and to play Huckleberry Finn in a long running radio adaptation of 'Tom Sawyer.' There cannot have been many Huckleberry Finns with a Geordie accent.

At the time RAF Transport Command in the Far East flew its Dakotas from Singapore to Adelaide in South Australia for servicing. One went every month and the crew returned with the one that had gone the previous month.

There was room aboard the Dakotas for Service passengers, provided:

a) that you were entitled to leave, and

b) that you had a permit to go signed by Brigadier A (for Admin).

I was entitled to twenty-eight days leave. And now I had a signed permit. The rest was routine. Three days later I was aboard a lame Dakota taking it in easy stages – Surabaya, Timor, Darwin, Alice Springs – to Adelaide.

Twenty-eight idyllic days were followed by twenty-eight clouded days. The monthly Dakota, after the one that had brought me, failed to turn up. So, fifty-six days after leaving Singapore I arrived back in Changi Airport one steaming Saturday afternoon and was immediately put under arrest.

My case in my own defence and my subsequent acquittal when faced with the charge of absenting myself without leave for twenty-eight days made legal history, albeit unrecorded until now, but that is another story.

I recount the incident of that autumn leave only to confront myself with that streak of recklessness in my character which is often unsuspected.

I am not a raver. I do not enroll in publicised adventures. I am not given to riotous assembly, I do not insult waiters or write begging letters. I have never beaten my wife and rarely chastised my children. And I am kind to cats.

But I am reckless. And my kind of recklessness has the propensity of caprice. It is subject to uncertainty. It is of a kind not to be confused with the customary taking of risks, which is scarcely a risky business at all. Risks are almost always calculated even if the calculations are inexact. The consequences of the risk-taking are always predictable, even if they are not always measurable.

Indeed, much risk-taking is little more than a breaking of the rules in the expectation of not being found out. To win is to outwit. To lose is to be caught. It is an activity without mystery and without honour.

And even the honourable gambler always knows in advance the consequences of his action. He will either win or lose. And deep down he probably hopes to lose. But there is no uncertainty.

A coin tossed will always fall either heads or tails. But I want to toss the coin which, as it spins in the air, will change into a tram ticket to an unknown destination.

My kind of recklessness is a taking of risks not as an act of defiance nor of assault but of whim and of fancy. It is a step into the unknown. And the results can be very engaging.

Once, in a cheery effort to make conversation with the chairman of a newspaper publishing group, I enquired who was destined to succeed an aging editor.

'It is a difficult problem,' he said. 'There is no one.' 'What about me?' I heard myself say, 'You have just solved a difficult problem,' he said, thereby sentencing me to six years of pushing a chapel uphill.

Fame, in that instance, was the spur of the moment.

A passion for what suddenly takes the fancy has been attributed by psychologists to premature birth. And curiously I was a premature baby. Eager to be born in the Twenties rather than the Thirties, I arrived three weeks early with three days to spare. On Holy Innocents' Day, no less. I was rather taken aback, I recall.

But a more likely explanation, if one is needed, of the recklessness of the non-raver is to see it as an attribute of the only child. And I am one of those also. The selfishness of the only child is not the selfishness of taking from others but the selfishness of completeness in isolation. And suddenly to act upon a whim is a reflection not of dissatisfaction but of wonder. It is aspiring not despairing.

Just suppose – is its emblem. What if? – is its motive.

The only child is an island entire of itself, and that island, as the poet said, is, 'Full of noises, sounds and sweet airs that give delight and hurt not.'

Even when taking risks.

September 1993

Know Your
Place

October is the first month of the year: the political year. MPs return from the recess, enjoy or endure their party conferences, and then re-assemble in Westminster. This year, in these troubled times, they will, I hope, be inspired by a truth which I can never resist reminding them of. We are the only country in Europe, with a population of more than 50 million, which has not lapsed into fascism or communism this century.

I know we are lucky. We live on an island and have not been seriously invaded for more than nine centuries. But we are politically astute. We cut off the king's head at the right moment. I once asked Christopher Hill, the historian, if Charles I deserved to have his head cut off.

That, he replied is a question only God could answer. But had I been there I would have voted for it.

In truth, we sorted out the constitution before we had the industrial revolution. To attempt a political revolution and an industrial revolution simultaneously is to court disaster, as Russia is now discovering.

But then we do not expect too much of politicians. We do not go round saluting them. Our system is very sensible. We have one lot, and when they look weary and perplexed, we have the other lot. And we are seldom disappointed.

We have confidence in the continuity of our history.

R. J. White, my favourite historian, and the author of the best Short History of England, taught me that more than forty years ago, when I was a student.

He would quote his favourite historian, Edmund Burke, who described that continuity as the happy effect of following nature in the conduct of the state.

And notice, no capital S for state.

Mr White himself argued that in this country the debate goes on, and the pace of progress, while it may be impeded by procrastination, is never wrecked upon the rocks of revolutionary cataclysm or wrenched in the embittering rapids of civil war.

One of the consequences, he said, of the habitual conservatism of our style of politics – a style which informs all parties alike when they exchange opposition for authority – is the happy absence of irreconcilables.

As long ago as the mid-eighteenth century, he wrote, English Tories learnt in the hard school of experience that the cost of Jacobitism (support for James II and his Stuart descendants) was political futility.

By the mid-twentieth century, he wrote, they have learnt the same lesson about opposition to planning and the welfare state.

But, I now have to ask, in the late twentieth century, have they and the other lot, and we, all forgotten that lesson?

Another Cambridge historian, Herbert Butterfield, once wrote that it is seldom the case in this country that the measures of one party (when it has its turn in office) are reversed because a general election produces a change in government.

Is that still true, and should it not be?

Politics is the art of the possible. The only moral criterion of a political act is its consequence, not the motive which inspired it. Harold Macmillan made the point unforgettably in an interview on television one evening shortly after his retirement. Asked what had worried him most during his time as Prime Minister he thought for a moment, and then replied: Events.

Politics is not about problems which can be solved but about difficulties which can be overcome. And as the politician sets out to overcome them, he or she discovers others which have just been created by the actions just taken.

That is why the politicians most to be avoided are those who talk of final solutions. That is the ultimate delusion of power.

There is much to be said for separating the functions of the Head of State and the Head of Government, which is the

234

principal virtue of our constitution and the explicit reason why we must not become a republic.

Let us keep our politicians in their place. They must not get above themselves.

October 1993

A Box is a
Box is a Box

Why, the little one asked her grandmother, does Grandpa say: Thank you for my Christmas box, and not: Thank you for my Christmas present? His present was not even in a box.

Grandma thought for a moment. Because he lives in the past, she said.

Grandpa smiled and lifted the little one on to his lap.

Once upon a time, he said, everbody's Christmas present came out of a box. And everybody got their present on the day after Christmas Day, which is why it is called Boxing Day.

And did everyone fight over their presents, asked the little one's older brother.

No, said Grandpa, no one even got their ears boxed.

His grandson grinned.

Grandpa went on to explain that there were collection boxes in every church and people would put their Christmas offerings in them. The contents were called the box money, or sometimes the dole of the Christmas box.

David's daddy is on the dole said his grandson. But Grandpa went on.

The boxes were opened on Christmas Day, he said, and then the box money would be distributed to the poor by the priests on the following day.

The postman and the dustman still get a Christmas box, said his grandson.

Precisely so, said Grandpa.

But my sister is right, said the boy: box seems to have two meanings – the container and the contents.

His grandfather looked at him fondly. Box, he said, has many meanings.

Detecting the start of a dissertation. Grandma picked up the little one and headed upstairs.

Grandpa reached for his dictionary.

Box, he said, is one of the most interesting words in the language. It can be a noun, or a verb, or an adjective; an object, or an act, or a description.

It can be many things. A rigid container with four sides and a bottom. A penalty area on a football pitch. A shield to protect the private parts of cricketers. A structure that contains a telephone to be used only by the police. A mobile conveyor for a horse. An office where you purchase tickets for the theatre.

You can have a box bed, a box camera, a box number, a box pew, a box spanner, a box spring, a box stall, and boxwood.

You can also be a boxer, said his grandson, clenching his fists.

Quite so, said Grandpa, even if you are a dog.

Oh yes, the German boxers, said his grandson. But who were the Chinese Boxers?

They, said Grandpa, were members of a Chinese secret society who were opposed to foreign influence in China, and whose rebellion was suppressed in 1900. Did you know that their name was an approximate translation of a Chinese word meaning righteous, harmonious fist.

Did they punch the air? said the grandson.

Grandpa chortled. No, he said, but they boxed the compass.

I thought the wind did that.

It can said Grandpa, when it blows from every quarter in rapid succession. But the expression is a nautical phrase meaning to name the thirty-two points of the compass in their correct order.

His grandson began to recite.

Hush, said Grandpa. Did you know that Sir Walter Raleigh once boxed his son's ears during an argument over dinner.

Not wishing to strike his father back, young Walter hit the man sitting on the other side of him, and said 'Box about, 'twill come to my father anon.'

Clearly he hoped that the blow should travel right round the dinner table and get back to his father. His remark became a proverb in the seventeenth century.

But what about Box and Cox, said his grandson, did they knock each other about?

No, replied his Grandpa, they probably never met. They lodged with a deceitful landlady called Mrs Bouncer, who let the same room to them. Unknown to each other they occupied it alternately, because one was out at work all day, and the other at work all night.

At that moment Grandma returned having put the little one to bed.

I wonder, she said, if there is anything on the box tonight.

November/December 1993

Brief Encounter

M y New Year resolution, said the old gentleman, is to write my memoirs. For publication? I asked. No, he replied, for my grandchildren and their children. Though I am a man of Letters. At that moment his wife interrupted him. He is pulling your leg, she said to me; what he means is that he has had a letter published in *Letters*, Saga's new magazine. And I think it has gone to his head.

The old gentleman laughed. It was better than a mini-saga, he said.

It was now my turn to laugh. You remember them? I said.

Of course, he said, you used to read them out loud on the Today programme. Every one was precisely fifty words.

He then astounded me by reciting the one I wrote. I had called it: Gone to hell – back shortly. And it read:

> *Afterwards he knew that it had all been a mistake.*
> *It ought never to have been allowed to happen. Being*
> *born was no joke. Growing up no pleasure. Growing*
> *old even worse. As he tried to tell them. And death*
> *when it came seemed like a blessed relief. Until*
> *afterwards . . .*

He paused. Our vicar used it as the text for a sermon, he said.

I looked at his wife. Now he is pulling my leg, I said. She grinned. He's wicked, she said, but I think he is serious about writing his memoirs. Or at least writing them down.

This encounter, like much of my social life, took place on the concourse of Euston railway station. I had never met the couple before but in the few minutes before we caught our separate trains, I urged the old gentleman to write his memoirs. Your grandchildren, I am sure, I said, will be enthralled by them.

I was still thinking about that encounter when I received a copy of a book called *I Can Fly*, published by Age Concern in Newcastle.

It is an anthology of the work of *Write Away*, a group of elderly people who meet regularly to share their common interest: creative writing.

In her foreword to the book, Margaret Forster says: When I was a child I used to plague first my grandparents and then my parents to tell me about what I liked to call 'the olden days'. I longed to know about their childhoods, about what the world was like when they were young. None of them was very good at satisfying my curiosity, and I'd bully and push them; sometimes, haltingly, they'd manage to recreate a brief part of their past. But it was never enough, and I always knew that they had in them a vast storehouse of memories which I was failing to tap.

And she goes on, very rightly, to commend the work of Julie Ward who runs *Write Away*.

I read all the pieces in the book on a train journey north and it was like going home to my childhood. It confirmed me in my belief that everyone has a tale to tell, given the opportunity.

I once interviewed on tape a number of mill girls in Lancashire, all of them old enough to recall life in the mills before the First World War. Schoolchildren who listened to the tapes were entranced.

And I know another school which decided to create a museum of the First World War and grandmothers donated letters which had been sent to them from boyfriends in the Somme.

Taping your memories may seem the soft option, less of a labour than writing, but imagine the joy of listening to your grandfather years after his death.

I have a friend, now hard at work at what he calls his recollections, who believes that the very act of remembering and recording, whether by the written word or the spoken word, is adding to his own understanding of life.

I am not being a historian, nor a philosopher, he says. I am not trying to be wise after the event. And I am certainly not writing fiction. But in remembering what happened, I am getting a clearer understanding of why it happened. I do not intend to bore my grandchildren with accounts of 'what if'. . . but I hope that they, too, will understand the importance of events in our lives.

He is a man who has always kept a diary, a modest diary, a simple record of events. I imagined that that would make his task easier, but he says not. The more he thinks about the past, he says, the more he realises that the really interesting bits never got in the diary.

He is scornful of those who keep detailed diaries and then publish them as memoirs: he dismisses that as an exercise in public relations.

The best source of your past, he says, are other people. He spent a weekend last year with a friend whom he had not seen since they were in the same class at school at the age of eight.

In one long conversation, which went on into the early hours, they both recalled people and events which both believed they had long since forgotten.

Both agreed that they had not enjoyed themselves as much for a long time. And my friend observed that he had come to the conclusion that the medieval friars were right. To recollect is not simply to recall memory, but to absorb in mystical contemplation.

Happy New Year.

January 1994

Playing With Words

I think of myself as a man of letters, but I have never solved a crossword puzzle. I suffer from what can only be called crucifixia – crossword blindness. And I have lived among crosswords all my life.

For several years, when I was Northern Editor of the *Guardian*, I had, as it were, the oversight of the paper's crosswords.

The crossword editor operated, like me, in Manchester, and every Friday he would present me with proofs of all the crosswords for the coming week, and all the answers.

He would point out a clue. Then he would point out the answer. And he would explain how he got from one to the other.

And I never understood a word he said.

Of course I gave up trying to solve crosswords a long time ago, but I have never ceased to marvel at the casually absorbed skill of those who can.

Once at a party to launch a new motor car – it was the Bentley S and I kept wondering if its successor would be the T model – I watched a man complete The Times Crossword in five minutes.

It was, he complained, getting too easy.

And on television I once refereed a contest between two crossword setters – they sound like angry dogs in the sunset – who swopped clues and answers with the speed of crosstalk comedians.

Inward hush – a snake in the skiffle group.

Washboard. Of course.

It is not as if I am indifferent to words, head-on or edgeways. I fondle them frequently, try them for size, sport them for a day or two, and then look elsewhere.

My favourite word is precisely, precisely because it is so

accurate. And over the years I have had love affairs with adjectives as distant as craven and vainglorious.

I like words to pop up unexpectedly but unerringly in sentences.

Alastair Cooke, a *Manchester Guardian* man, wrote of an American senator who was halfway through a vote of thanks when – as Cooke put it – 'his teleprompter went on the blink and he was compelled to speak from the heart.'

Compelled. The precise word.

To some men of letters words are slippery, like goldfish, difficult to grasp, now one thing now the other.

To others they are concrete, sharpedged as diamonds, absolute as the *Oxford English Dictionary*.

I'm an *OED* man myself. I have the compact edition photographed down into two volumes and I peer at it through an eyeglass like an Amsterdam jeweller.

Do I look for meaning or spelling?

Neither.

I look, like a man looking in a mirror, for confirmation.

A word is more than an arrangement of letters, more than a definition, more than an articulated sound.

It is a small world inside the big world that is language. It is a universal reminder, a key to understanding.

I am the Word, He said. And that was putting it in a word. You can deduce the whole universe from the right word.

But not all the time.

There are workaday words. Pass the salt. Pass along the car. Pass the word. And there are words as playthings – to be linked, to be teased, to be crossed.

That I suspect is the addiction of the crossword – a desire to play with words, not to bask in the recollection they evoke, not even to respond to the images they record, but to play a game with them, like picking daisies to make chains.

It is as if words were molecules and crosswords were an excuse for re-arranging the atoms.

Water is wet and cool to the poet, drink to the recluse, H_2O to the chemist, and five letters to the man who fills in the crossword. A crossword is an abstraction, all association and no emotion. It neither translates nor transcends.

It is a law unto itself. And I think of those who daily practise that law as men assured.

They are people of regular habits, confident that the sun will rise again in the morning, and that the answer to 16 across will prove to have been a misprint.

I see them set in their ways – disciplined and organised. They are not haunted by the thought that they should be somewhere else, or someone else.

Instead they sit, steadily filling in those small squares.

Old priest starts upsetting Levite with needless oath.

Expletive.

What else?

Omniscient as Sherlock Holmes they share a daily exchange with an anonymous but so familiar, so well understood, creator.

The world of the crossword is a cosy and a brittle world, which can be tidied away and brought out again tomorrow.

He who does a crossword sets off each day on a journey into the known, not the unknown. He travels hopefully and he almost always arrives.

In a word, the crossword is the private language of the commuter.

I find it adumbrating.

Or to put it another way.

A silent sailor sketching.

February 1994